ALASKA

A Challenge in Conservation

A CONSERVATION FOUNDATION STUDY

ALASKA

A CHALLENGE IN CONSERVATION

RICHARD A. COOLEY

THE UNIVERSITY OF WISCONSIN PRESS

MADISON, MILWAUKEE, AND LONDON, 1967

Published by

The University of Wisconsin Press

Madison, Milwaukee, and London

U.S.A.: Box 1379, Madison, Wisconsin 53701

U.K.: 26–28 Hallam Street, London W.1

First printing (cloth), 1966

Second printing (paper), 1967

Printed in the United States of America

Library of Congress Catalog Card Number 66–13799

To Alice, Brig, and Matt

Foreword

WHEN Alaska attained statehood in 1958, Congress authorized the new state to select 104 million acres of unreserved federal land over the next twenty-five years. The future of the rich and largely untapped natural resources of Alaska—forest, minerals, water sources, wildlife, and magnificent scenery—will depend on policies adopted for selection, classification and disposition of this vast acreage. What will be the criteria for selection? What are the economic and social consequences of alternative programs?

Richard Cooley is a resource economist who has pursued research in Alaska for the Conservation Foundation for many years. He is no *chechako*. He loves Alaska for its varied and magnificent environment, its mountains, glaciers, lakes, and streams. He understands the economic and political problems statehood presents and he knows much about the ambitions and hopes of the people. He appreciates the inevitability of industrial development and population increase, and is fully aware of the history of resource exploitation and destruction in the development of other western states. He is mindful of the patchwork land-use policies and programs that caused so much distress in that earlier process of progress.

In this book Dr. Cooley presents in lay language the problems and issues facing the people of Alaska in molding their own future. He considers, in terms of modern theories of land management, the mistakes of the past. At the same time he recognizes that Alaska is unique and that it will face problems different in scope and degree from other regions in earlier times. He anticipates the conflict that will arise between the need for immediate revenue and the need for long-range conservation of natural resources. Paramount is the need for informed planning and development of the total environment for sustained prosperity of both the land and the people. In Alaska, time is of the essence.

This is a book of values that will have impact far beyond the borders of Alaska. Congress has recently established a Public Land Law Review Commission to undertake the herculean task of revising and updating federal land policies. It is high time for most of the states to do the same with their own antiquated hodge-podge of local land laws and practices. The elements of planning so clearly and fully presented in this book are relevant and important everywhere to what President Johnson has called the evolution of the "new conservation" for a Great Society. Land use for environmental health *is* the new conservation.

Here is exciting analysis; for the book deals with causes and consequences and, ultimately, ways of life. Quality is as important as quantity in the development of the land for enduring prosperity. Cooley, the economist, understands this: land-use planning can and should be practical and spiritual as well. As an economist, conservationist and writer, he makes this evident between the lines. He has written of the land and its use with love and fear; we hope, before it is too late.

SAMUEL H. ORDWAY, JR.

New York, N.Y.

Contents

	FOREWORD	vii
	INTRODUCTION	3
1	NORTH COUNTRY	7
2	POLITICS AND THE STATE PATRIMONY	18
3	A NEW POLICY FOR LAND USE	32
4	LAND OFFICE BUSINESS	48
5	DEVELOPMENT VS. CONSERVATION	63
6	PATTERNS OF SETTLEMENT	73
7	CONFLICTS IN RESOURCE USE	83
8	INTERAGENCY AND JURISDICTIONAL CONFLICTS	96
9	PLANNING AND THE POLITICAL STRUGGLE	108
10	A CONSERVATION ETHIC	118
	MAPS	132
	APPENDIX TABLES	147
	BIBLIOGRAPHY	157
	INDEX	161

Illustrations

PLATES

following page 80

Yentna Glacier, cutting south through the rugged Alaska Range

Despite its barren appearance, the arctic provides subsistence for Eskimo and wildlife alike

Dense forests of spruce and hemlock in the Tongass National Forest

Geese and other migratory birds on the Chickaloon flats

Bears are the least able of all big game to withstand the spread of settlement

Whiteface Herefords on Kodiak Island

New techniques greatly reduce the time and cost of surveys in Alaska

New highway near Anchorage

Shantytowns have sprung up on the edges of Alaska's cities

Oil refinery on the Kenai Peninsula

Abandoned military base in the Aleutian Islands

The alpine tundra provides a unique wilderness experience

A canoe trail in the Kenai National Moose Range

FIGURES

Figure 1 Federal Land Grants to States 26

Figure 2 Organization of the Division of Lands 36

MAPS

Map 1 Physiographic Provinces of Alaska 133
Map 2 Major Population Centers of Alaska 134
Map 3 Boundaries of Organized Boroughs 135
Map 4 Transportation Routes 136
Map 5 Major Federal Land Reserves 137
Map 6 State Land Selections 138
Map 7 Native Land Claims 139
Map 8 Generalized Agricultural Areas of Alaska 140
Map 9 Forests of Alaska 141
Map 10 Critical Big Game Areas: Goat, Sheep, and Bear 142
Map 11 Critical Big Game Areas: Moose and Caribou 143
Map 12 Major Waterfowl and Fish Areas 144
Map 13 Better Known Mineral Deposits and Petroleum Provinces 145
Map 14 Potential Mineral Areas 146

Tables

TEXT TABLES

1 Land Status in Alaska 23
2 Federal Land Grants to Alaska 28
3 Alaska's Population Growth 64

APPENDIX TABLES

A. Revenue from State Lands, 1959–64 147
B. Total State Revenues from State and Federal Lands and Resources, 1959–64 148
C. Total Operating Costs of the Division of Lands, 1959–64 149
D. Total Net Operating Costs of the Division of Lands Compared with Total Recurrent Income from State Lands, 1959–64 149
E. Recurrent and Non-Recurrent Revenues from State Lands, 1959–64 150
F. Revenues from State Lands by Types of Grants and Resources, 1959–64 151
G. State Land Selection Progress, 1959–64 152
H. Annual Income from Upland Leases and Sales, 1961–64 153
I. Competitive Oil and Gas Leasing of State Lands, 1959–64 154
J. Non-Competitive Oil and Gas Leasing of State Lands, 1959–64 155
K. Federal Revenue Payments to the State of Alaska for Oil, Gas, and Coal Leasing on Federal Lands, 1959–64 156
L. Timber Sales and Harvests from State Lands, 1959–64 156

ALASKA
A Challenge in Conservation

Introduction

ONE of the largest land transactions in the history of the nation is taking place in Alaska today. With passage of the Statehood Act in 1958, Alaska was given the right to select approximately 104 million acres from the federal public domain. Nearly one-third of the total area of the state, or an area larger than California, this grant represents the transfer of an empire. Never before has Congress been so liberal in providing a land patrimony for a newly formed state of the Union.

In the selection, management, and disposal of these lands, Alaska is undertaking a pioneering effort. No other state has had quite the same opportunity to conceive and carry out a rational land program on such a gigantic scale. Alaska is beginning with a relatively unspoiled environment. Its magnificent scenic, wildlife, and wilderness resources are largely intact, and there has been no complicated pattern of land settlement and development. And it has embarked on its land program at a time when knowledge of the principles of land management and conservation is far greater than it was when the West was the last frontier. Can the state of Alaska learn from past mistakes in other areas?

Seven years have elapsed since the state launched its land program. Changes have been spectacular. Laws setting forth state land and resource policies have been enacted; an administrative agency has been created to implement constitutional and statutory provisions; and policies for the selection, classification, and disposal of state lands have been designed and put into effect. By 1966, the state land program had taken its basic shape and the great transfer of lands from federal to state and private ownership was well under way. Developments have occurred so rapidly that few people other than those directly involved in the program are aware of the size and significance of the decisions being made. The stakes are huge, and precipitate action could easily lead to results which the people of Alaska and the nation as a whole would regret in the years to come.

This is one of a series of related studies supported by the Conservation Foundation dealing with the problems and the potentialities of resource development in Alaska. In 1952, at the request of the Secretary of the Interior, the Foundation completed an independent analysis of the Department's many important natural resource program activities and policies in the territory. The study was carried out under the leadership of the Foundation's recently retired president, Samuel H. Ordway, Jr. Many basic changes have taken place in Alaska since that date, yet a number of the Foundation's conclusions and recommendations are still highly pertinent.

> The kind of responsible venture capital and responsible free enterprise greatly needed now will be attracted to Alaska only as more knowledge becomes available of environmental conditions, the location and extent of resources, and the opportunities and risks of development.
>
> Mapping, surveying, inventorying and research of all kinds have been allowed to lag far behind present needs. The land disposal policy and program is fraught with uncertainty, red tape and delay. . . .
>
> Integration and coordination of the planning and programming of many diverse federal and Territorial agencies is imperative.
>
> A national policy for the development of Alaska should be adopted—aimed toward an economy of sustained resource management, and continuing productivity—not quick exploitation.
>
> A plan for the study of Alaska's resources, area by area, by teams of technicians familiar with *all* resources, not by separate agencies separately, should be adopted. Then should follow zoning of regions for optimum land use, and then should follow disposal of these properly studied and classified areas for such optimum or multiple use. The Federal Government

should not be stampeded into rapid disposal of land and resources without knowledge of their potentials.

An Alaska Planning Commission should be immediately established . . . to meet the needs and implement policies recommended in this Report.

Alaska remains a vital, under-developed area, essential to the defense and economy of the United States, and should receive federal aid and assistance commensurate with its large land area and resource potential in far greater amounts than aid is now going to under-developed foreign lands.[1]

Had more been accomplished toward the fulfillment of these recommendations during the 1950's, the state today would not be confronted with so many difficult and complex policy issues in the launching of its land program.

In the following years the Conservation Foundation undertook other major resource policy studies. These included: an ecological reconnaissance of Alaska, concerning the impact of human settlement on wildlife habitats, conducted by two eminent biologists; [2] a special study of public policy relating to the potentialities for outdoor recreation in Alaska, completed for the Outdoor Recreation Resources Review Commission; [3] an analysis of Alaska's population and economic growth with projections of future trends, completed under a contract with the State Department of Economic Development and Planning; [4] an examination of the political, social, economic, and biological factors involved in the conservation of Alaska's salmon resources; [5] and an assessment of the quality and quantity of Alaska's land resources and of

1. "Alaska Program Analysis," prepared for the U.S. Department of the Interior by the Conservation Foundation, February 1, 1952 (mimeo), pp. ii–iii.

2. A. Starker Leopold and F. Fraser Darling, *Wildlife in Alaska: An Ecological Reconnaissance.* New York: The Ronald Press, 1953.

3. Wallace D. Bowman, *Alaska's Outdoor Recreation Potential,* A Report to the Outdoor Recreation Resources Review Commission by the Conservation Foundation (ORRRC Study Report No. 9), Washington, D.C., 1962.

4. George W. Rogers and Richard A. Cooley, *Alaska's Population and Economy: Regional Growth, Development and Future Outlook,* Report to the Department of Economic Development and Planning, 1962 (2 vols.). Published by University of Alaska Economic Series, Institute of Business, Economic and Government Research, 1963.

5. Richard A. Cooley, *Politics and Conservation: The Decline of the Alaska Salmon.* New York: Harper & Row, 1963.

their national significance.[6] For over a decade the Conservation Foundation has shown an abiding interest in the unique problems and unusual opportunities in the development and conservation of Alaska's magnificent natural resources.

The degree to which Alaska succeeds in managing and developing its valuable land estate will depend to a large extent upon public understanding of the issues at stake, and it is hoped that this review and analysis of the state program will contribute toward that end. How the state handles this important responsibility will be a major factor in determining the quality and character of both life and the landscape in Alaska for decades to come.

6. Hugh A. Johnson and Harold T. Jorgenson, *The Land Resources of Alaska.* New York: University Publishers, 1963.

Chapter 1

North Country

THERE are over 365 million acres of land in Alaska, an area larger than the five western states of Washington, Oregon, California, Arizona, and Nevada. It is the largest peninsula in the Western Hemisphere, with a coastline of nearly 34,000 miles. The southernmost point is about 600 miles north of the State of Washington. Near Point Barrow in the Arctic, the northern tip is only about 1,250 miles from the North Pole. To the west, 56 miles across the Bering Strait, is Siberia which thousands of years ago was connected to Alaska by a land bridge, and today Russians on Big Diomede Island and Americans on Little Diomede Island can almost shout greetings to each other. The rugged and treeless Aleutian Islands reach westward into the Pacific Ocean, like steppingstones across a pond, to within a thousand miles of Japan.

Shortly after Secretary of State William H. Seward retired from office a friend asked, "What do you consider the most important measure of your career?" "The purchase of Alaska," Seward replied, "but it will take the people a generation to find out."[1] That many did not consider the purchase in 1867 a great real estate bargain is evident from congressional debates and newspaper articles of that time. The purchase price of $7,200,000 was denounced as a reckless waste of taxpayers' money, and the

1. H. H. Bancroft, *History of Alaska, 1730–1885* (New York: Antiquarian Press, reprint 1959), p. 747.

territory was portrayed as a barren wasteland of ice and snow. Walrussia, Icebergia, Polaria, Seward's Icebox, and Seward's Folly were only a few of the contemptuous epithets then freely applied and the image persisted a remarkably long time. Contrast this with the views expressed by Henry Gannett, for many years the Chief Geographer for the Geological Survey and a member of the Alaska Harriman expedition near the turn of the century. After extolling the possibilities he foresaw for the development of Alaska's resources, Gannett concluded:

> There is one other asset of the territory not yet enumerated; imponderable and difficult to appraise, yet one of the chief assets of Alaska, if not the greatest. This is the scenery. There are glaciers, mountains, fiords elsewhere, but nowhere else on earth is there such abundance and magnificence of mountain, fiord and glacier scenery. For thousands of miles the coast is a continuous panorama. For one Yosemite of California, Alaska has hundreds. The mountains and glaciers of the Cascade Range are duplicated and a thousandfold exceeded in Alaska. The Alaska coast is to become the show place of the entire earth, and pilgrims not only from the United States but from beyond the seas will throng in endless procession to see it. Its grandeur is more valuable than the gold or the fish, or the timber, for it will never be exhausted. This value measured by direct returns in money from tourists will be enormous; measured in health and pleasure it will be incalculable.[2]

The pendulum of opinion about what Alaska is or can be has swung wildly back and forth from optimism to pessimism during the hundred years since its purchase; and today one still finds many contrasting views about this land and what the future may hold for it. The differences spring in part from the differing philosophies, desires, and yearnings of the people who have come north to populate Alaska, but they also reflect its enormous size and the great diversity of its natural and physical features, which make generalization about the future extraordinarily difficult. The inadequate knowledge of the land and its resources has greatly aggravated this state of affairs.

2. Henry Gannett, "General Geography," *Harriman Alaska Expedition,* Vol. II (New York: Doubleday Page Co., 1904), pp. 276–77.

Physical geography has played a major role in the history and economic development of the region, and no one can fully understand the problems of the past or properly evaluate the future without at least a general understanding of these natural characteristics. The basic land forms and physical features described below have challenged man's ingenuity from the beginning and will continue to influence the pattern of development and settlement in the future. (A list of references of the principal published works on the subject has been included in the bibliography.)

Three great mountain ranges present the most prominent topographic feature of Alaska. The mountains of the continental United States are arranged in roughly north-south trends, while those of Alaska occur in broad arcs with prevalent east-west trends. The Coast Range is part of a continuous mountain system extending northward from Washington State along the west coast of British Columbia into southeastern Alaska. The mountains continue in an arc along the Gulf of Alaska into the Kenai Peninsula and reappear from the sea as Kodiak Island at the southern tip. Along the entire southern coast, steep mountain slopes rise directly from the sea, with peaks as high as 19,850 feet in the St. Elias mountains. This formidable edge of the continent is indeed picturesque but presents natural barriers to transportation and communication which have handicapped development of the hinterlands and profoundly affected the life of the area. Many of the high mountain regions are covered by ice fields, the source of large glaciers that often reach down to the sea. One of the largest, Malaspina Glacier on the Gulf of Alaska, is bigger than the state of Rhode Island. These valley glaciers have gouged and sharpened the contours of the coastal mountains, leaving many steep-walled fiords where the water is deep enough for ocean steamers. A few of the fiords and river valleys provide pathways through the mountains giving occasional points of access to the land beyond. Such a one is Cook Inlet where two major rivers, the Susitna and the Matanuska, can be followed upstream deep into the interior.

Further inland and cutting across central Alaska is the mighty Alaska Range, about six hundred miles long, containing a number of famous peaks including the highest in North America, Mount McKinley, which rises to 20,320 feet. Merging into the coastal mountains at its eastern end, it serves at its western end as the backbone of the Alaska Peninsula and Aleutian Islands. The granite peaks of the Alaska Range are snow-covered throughout the year, and glaciers cut southward to the lowlands. Despite its rugged character the Alaska Range can be crossed more easily than the Coast Range, for there are many major river valleys providing routes of travel. The Alaska Railroad from Seward at tidewater to Fairbanks in the interior follows the Nenana River while the Richardson Highway from Valdez to Fairbanks follows the Delta River through the Alaska Range.

Least known and explored is the Brooks Range tending east-west from the Canadian border across northern Alaska. It is a continuation of the Rocky Mountains, and cuts an arc in reverse from the other two, ending near Point Hope on the Arctic Ocean. Its entire length of about six hundred miles is above the Arctic Circle. The loftiest peaks are not far from the Alaska-Canada border where mounts Chamberlain and Michelson rise to around ten thousand feet. A number of large rivers emerge from the Brooks Range: the Koyukuk flowing southwesterly into the Yukon River; the Kobuk and Noatak flowing westerly into Bering Strait near Kotzebue; and the Colville flowing north into the Arctic Ocean. Many blue-green glacier lakes are scattered through its ranges. By virtue of its inaccessibility and its arctic environment, the Brooks Range is one of the most valuable of the few large wilderness areas remaining in the United States.

To the south of the Brooks Range is the great Yukon Basin. Known more commonly as interior Alaska, the Basin is bordered on the south by the Alaska Range and contains the drainages of the Yukon and Kuskokwim rivers. The Yukon is the third largest river in North America, exceeded only by the Mississippi and the Mackenzie. Over 2,400 miles long, it rises in northern British Columbia and flows northwest into Alaska where it traces a broad arc for some 1,500 miles in a westerly and then southwesterly direction before emptying into the Bering Sea. During and following the gold rush, the river served as a major artery of transportation to the interior and the Klondike in Yukon Territory. The Basin is roughly funnel-shaped with the interior lowlands and plains (the Yukon flats) forming the narrower portion in the northeast near the Canadian border, and the deltas of the Yukon and Kuskokwim rivers in southwestern Alaska constituting the broader mouth along the shores of the Bering Sea. It is a vast land of low relief containing large bands of permafrost (i.e., permanently frozen ground), muskeg, tundra, and thousands upon thousands of small shallow lakes.

North of the Brooks Range lies the true arctic. Covering about one-sixth of the total area of Alaska, it consists predominantly of low rolling hills and plateaus dissected by northward flowing rivers and streams draining into the polar seas. Most of the area is covered with permanently frozen tundra. This remote region no doubt was the image of Alaska most people held in the days when it was known as Seward's Icebox.

The climate of Alaska is as variable as the topography by which it is strongly influenced. Along the southern coastal area, the warm ocean currents and the moisture-laden winds from the south combine to give the region a marine climate much like that of Washington and Oregon. Precipitation is extremely heavy since little moisture is able to penetrate beyond the coastal mountain barrier; but temperatures are warm throughout the year. The city of Juneau, for example, has an annual precipitation of around sixty inches a year, summer temperatures like those of San Francisco, and mid-winter temperatures less severe than Chicago. There is, however, a heavy snowfall in the winter, and in the higher mountain areas along the coast there are immense annual accumulations that form the snow fields from which the great valley glaciers originate. On the other side of the Coast Range, the sea no longer has its moderating influence. The mildness of the climate declines rapidly, and it becomes subarctic in character, with much less precipitation and much greater seasonal variation in temperature. Around Fairbanks in interior Alaska annual precipitation is only about twelve inches a year. Summer temperatures rise to 100 degrees but winter brings some of the coldest weather recorded anywhere in North America, with temperatures as low as 75 degrees below zero in parts of the region.

These great extremes in temperatures are duplicated nowhere else in Alaska. Further north in the arctic region beyond the Brooks Range the climate is again moderated by the Bering Sea and the Arctic Ocean. At Point Barrow on the northern coast, for example, the precipitation is very low, amounting to less than five inches a year; the maximum summer temperature ever recorded is 78 degrees while the lowest winter temperature is —56 degrees. From late November until early February the residents of Point Barrow do not see the sun. Conversely, the sun never dips below the horizon throughout most of the summer months—a time of great activity in the arctic for all life. To a varying degree this is true of all Alaska. At Juneau in southeastern Alaska, the winter daylight at its peak lasts only about five or six hours, while in the summer there may be no darkness at all, only twilight for an hour or two.

The great contrasts in Alaska's climate are responsible to a large degree for the variety and abundance of the flora and fauna. The moderate temperature and heavy rainfall in the coastal mountains have produced dense forests of hemlock and spruce, with an equally dense understory of cedars, alders, mosses, blueberry bushes, devil's-club, and ferns, on the steep seaward slopes and up the river valleys. As a northern extension of the lush coastal rain forests of the Pacific Northwest, they encompass about 16 million acres of commercial timber land stretching in a narrow band along the entire southern coastline. The forests, meadows, and steep rocky slopes above the timber line support a wide variety of wildlife. Mountain goats range the high peaks. Sitka deer live on the islands along the coast, and both here and on the nearby mainland live brown, black, and grizzly bears, and timber wolves. Among the fur animals are mink, marten, land otters, wolverines, weasels, and a few beaver. A variety of trout live in the streams and lakes, and during the summer months the anadromous salmon swarm up the rivers and creeks to their spawning grounds. Halibut, seals, porpoises, sea lions, and whales are among the sea life along the coast, and grouse, ptarmigan, Steller's jay, golden and bald eagles, and many song birds are found.

Further northward in the region of the Alaska Range and the Yukon Plateau are the interior forests, covering an estimated 125 million acres of land. These are eastward extensions of the Canadian boreal forests containing black and white spruce, birch, aspen, cottonwood, and poplar. Stands are scattered and broken, and are limited to the better drained valley floors and the lower slopes of the mountain ranges. The trees frequently are small, and growth in general is slow as a result of the subarctic climate. This is a region of good range lands, with lichens and sedges and willows providing excellent browse for moose and caribou. Dall sheep, black, grizzly, and brown bears are to be found, and among the principal fur animals are lynx, fox, beaver, muskrat, marten, mink, wolverine, and weasel. Coyotes and timber wolves prey on the wildlife, and the snowshoe hare is as common as the cottontail is in Iowa. Reindeer, musk oxen, and buffalo have been introduced successfully in several locations.

The great delta of the Yukon and Kuskokwim rivers, and a huge expanse of lakes and tundra on the upper reaches of the Yukon—the Yukon flats—contain splendid areas for nesting waterfowl, including such migratory birds as Canadian and white-fronted geese, green-winged teal and the harlequin, pintail, and mallard ducks. Song birds are summer visitors, and grouse and willow ptarmigan are found on the uplands. Fish life includes arctic grayling, trout, and salmon, the latter being taken in large numbers primarily for subsistence purposes by the Indians and Eskimos. Marine mammals abound in the coastal waters of the Bering Sea, and valuable herds of Alaska fur seals haul out each year on the rocky shores of the Pribilof Islands, some two hundred miles out from the mainland. On the Aleutian Islands are immense colonies of sea birds, sea lion rookeries, and the remnants of a once abundant herd of sea otters, now slowly increasing as a result of government protection. Some of the finest grasslands in Alaska are to be found on the lower Alaska Peninsula and Aleutian Islands.

Beyond the Brooks Range in the arctic, caribou graze the windswept slopes and plateaus among the mosses, lichens, grasses, flowers, and dwarf willows which are induced to grow by the continuous sunshine from May until August. Ptarmigan, red foxes, timber wolves, weasels and occasionally grizzly bears range over the tundra and along the willow-bordered streams of the Arctic Slope. Timber is thin or wanting, and willows which frequently grow only a few inches high, spreading laterally over the ground, are the predominant tree life. Grayling, pike, and sheefish live in the streams; seal, walrus, and various species of whale in the Arctic Ocean. Along the coast and out on the offshore pack ice live the majestic polar bear with their entourage of white foxes. In spite of their barren appearance, these arctic lands have for centuries provided the subsistence needs of a sizable population of Eskimos. Though lying over permanently frozen ground and blanketed by snow, ice, and total darkness during the winter, the bleak tundra each year changes under the continuous summer sunlight into a beautiful carpet of miniature flowering plants.

Knowledge of the geology of Alaska and of the possibilities for developing its hidden resources is poor. In spite of long and extensive search for gold and other metals and minerals and more recently for oil and gas, the surface has been only scratched by modern prospecting techniques. There is geological information about the general types and extent of rocks, and mineral fuels and metallic mineralization are known to occur in many places, but thousands of square miles remain unexplored and hidden from view by the pervasive vegetation, permafrost, and other surface cover. Past production has been limited primarily to those minerals with a high unit value—gold, silver, copper, lead, zinc, and mercury. Mining was once the chief industry in Alaska but has gradually declined in importance. Discovery during the last few years, however, of major oil and gas deposits in the Cook Inlet region has touched off a boom in private oil exploration and development, and major companies are currently spending millions of dollars annually exploring other promising oil provinces throughout Alaska, going as far north as the Brooks Range and the Arctic Slope. Alaska today is producing oil in significant quantities, and geologists consider it one of the most promising petroleum regions of the world. Of the known mineral prospects, the more favorable—copper, iron, and coal—still await development. One large high-grade copper deposit is presently being developed on the Kobuk River in northwestern Alaska, and various large, low-grade iron ore deposits along the southern coast are under exploration. Some development of Alaska's mammoth deposits of coal has also occurred in the more accessible areas. Other important minerals found in varying quantities and qualities include tin, mercury, nickel, lead-zinc, antimony, chromite, molybdenum, tungsten, gold and silver, and various industrial and nonmetallic minerals.

There are two main reasons why such little progress has been made in developing these mineral resources. The first is purely economic: Alaska's northern location, rugged topography, and harsh climate have always made exploration and mining a very costly operation, and market conditions have been such that only the very highest grade properties can be worked. A second problem has been the ignorance of geological structures and a corresponding lack of data concerning mineral deposits. Good topographic maps have been published for most of the region, but geological mapping has lagged, and only about 15 percent of Alaska is now covered by published geological maps at a scale of four miles to the inch. These maps, and others of an even larger scale, are necessary for efficient private explorations of specific mineralized areas and to permit extrapolation of information to other unfamiliar areas with similar geologic structures. The development of the Alaska oil industry is an excellent example of the application of exploration methods based on geological similarities and probabilities. Alaska's rocks may well be as productive of minerals as their counterparts in neighboring Canada and the western United States; only more knowledge will tell, but the long-term prospects are encouraging.

These are Alaska's lands and resources—its natural endowment—sketched in very broad terms. There are over 100 million acres of commercial timber land; more than 60 million acres of potential grazing lands; some 2 or 3 million acres of land suitable for farming and other agricultural enterprises; large known and inferred reserves of oil and gas as well as deposits of various minerals awaiting more favorable conditions for exploration and development; great quantities of clear, unpolluted water; nearly 200 large potential hydroelectric sites with an estimated installed capacity of 20 million kilowatts; an incomparable array of birds, fish, mammals, and other wildlife resources on both land and water; one of the world's greatest untapped commercial fisheries off its coast; outstanding natural beauty and unsurpassable resources for outdoor recreation; and in this increasingly congested world where empty space has come to have important tangible values, Alaska has elbow room to spare.

Nature has been generous with Alaska. But a simple cataloguing of separate natural resources is deceiving. Knowledge of the nature and existence of natural resources is only one factor in development. Market demands, costs of production, the rate of technological change, a people's ideals and values, and the character of their political and social institutions also determine the pattern of natural resource use at any given time. Such natural resources moreover cannot be regarded as discrete categories. The harvest of one may destroy or preclude the use of another, and resources compete as alternative means of satisfying similar demands of society. Man is forced to make difficult choices between incompatible resource uses on the basis of his scale of values and his ethical standards. In the making of decisions, conflict and controversy are inevitable. The key to success in land policy lies not in seeking absolutes but in maintaining a flexible system which—by a constant appraisal and reappraisal of the practical effect of land and resource policies upon the long-run welfare of all the people—unrelentingly seeks the elusive, shifting public interest.

Chapter 2

Politics and the State Patrimony

THE purchase of the territory from Russia in 1867 was the last major land acquisition of the United States. It marked the end of a national era during which the federal government succeeded in acquiring public domain lands amounting to 1.8 billion acres, and it coincided with the unfolding of fundamental changes in national attitude toward the role and responsibility of the federal government in the ownership and management of public lands.

National land policies during the nineteenth century were predominantly concerned with disposal of the public domain for purposes of raising revenues, inducing agricultural settlement in the West, establishing new states, assisting the financing of school systems, and encouraging the construction of canals, roads, a transcontinental railway system, and other internal improvements. The federal government did little to protect and develop the land under its ownership or even to determine the nature and location of its resource wealth. The General Land Office viewed its function as facilitating the most rapid transfer of the areas within its control to private hands. Preference was nominally given to the establishment of permanent homes for farm families, but administrative practice also relinquished every type of resource—land, forests, minerals, and water power—to corporate interests as well.

By the late 1870's the nation had rid itself of a large portion of its public domain lands, and the era of the western frontier, when lands were cheap or free and resources were believed to be inexhaustible, was rapidly drawing to an end. During this period —only a few years after the Alaska acquisition—a strong reaction began to develop against these national disposal policies, for, although they had speeded settlement and development in the western United States, they had also resulted in unsavory land frauds, corrupt administration, speculation, monopoly, and the brutal waste and spoilation of natural resources. This was the genesis of the conservation movement; through the crusading zeal of Theodore Roosevelt, Gifford Pinchot, and others it grew into a national political cause at the beginning of the twentieth century. The movement had two main aspects with respect to land: great areas of the remaining public domain that contained resources of national significance were withdrawn and reserved for permanent government retention; and the federal government assumed responsibility on an unprecedented scale for land management, and began systematically surveying resources and planning for their interrelated development. During the next few decades, millions of acres of land were set aside for national forests, parks, wildlife refuges, and other public needs; and federal conservation policy was extended to include water resources, mineral extraction, timber production, recreation, wildlife protection, grazing, soil conservation, and eventually nearly every phase of natural resource use.

It has been the national land policies of this reservation era, rather than the earlier disposal policies, which have had a major impact upon Alaska and its unique pattern of land ownership.

The contrast between the federal land policies that guided the settlement and development of the West and those put forth for Alaska could hardly be greater. On October 24, 1867, just six days after the Alaska acquisition was officially consummated, the Secretary of the Interior announced that any attempt to claim lands in the territory under the land laws of the United States would be considered illegal; intruders would be removed by military force if necessary.[1] Seventeen years later, in the Alaska Organic Act of 1884, Congress extended the United States mining laws to Alaska (23 U.S. Stat., 24) and so made it possible to patent mining claims on the public domain. But not until the turn of the century, some thirty years after Alaska had come under American rule, could public lands be entered and patented for other purposes.

A wedge to open the way for agricultural settlement was forged in 1890 with the passage of a special act of Congress (30 U.S. Stat., 409) extending to Alaska the right to homestead public lands. It limited claims to eighty acres of surveyed lands and required homesteaders to pay the expenses of surveying. However, since no baselines for surveys existed and no provision was made for surveys, no settler was able to acquire title to land under the act. A few years later the law was amended to permit entry on 160 acres of surveyed or unsurveyed lands, but the amendment also included requirements for residency and cultivation in conformity with the national Homestead Act.[2] These requirements were not designed with Alaska's unique physical and economic conditions in mind, and few homesteaders were able to comply. As a result, very little land was transferred from public to private ownership under terms of the act. Under another act, the Trade and Manufacturing Sites Act passed in 1891 (26 U.S. Stat., 1095), a citizen or corporation could purchase small acreages of public land for the purpose of establishing a business enterprise. Its primary purpose was to provide means for corporations to obtain title to land for the establishment of salmon canneries, and it contained many safeguards to prevent its misuse for speculative endeavors. A site for a proposed business could not be patented, but only land actually occupied, and shown to be occupied in good faith. The maximum acreage was set at eighty acres, and to protect public access, no claim could extend more than one-fourth of a mile along the shore of any navigable waters.

1. 45th Cong., 15th Sess., Senate Document 59, p. 121.

2. 33 U.S. Stat., 1028, amended the original act to permit entry and patent of 320 acres, but this was reduced to 160 acres in 1916.

For many years these two acts provided the only mechanism for gaining title to public lands in Alaska. At wide intervals in later years other acts were passed making small tracts of land available for recreational and residential uses, for the leasing of grazing lands, and for the sale of timber and other materials from the public domain under government regulations. All of these laws contain various provisions to discourage the misappropriation of public lands for speculative purposes, but all are in need of modernization to meet existing conditions in Alaska.

In the western states the reservation era began only after a large portion of the best public lands with known resource values had already passed into private ownership. In Alaska, Congress, the President, and the many new federal resource agencies were free to withdraw and reserve large tracts of the choicest land for permanent government retention before any substantial development occurred. Shortly after the turn of the century all of the prime forest lands along Alaska's southern coast were withdrawn by executive order to create the Tongass and Chugach national forests, and other large areas of the most unusual natural beauty were set aside as national parks and monuments. In the years that followed further extensive tracts were reserved for wildlife refuges and ranges, Indian and military reserves, and a large number of smaller areas for navigation sites, potential hydroelectric installations, public recreation, and other miscellaneous government purposes. For the most part, none of these reserved lands were open to private entry and settlement. By an executive order in 1906, coal lands were also withdrawn from private location and entry, and no private development was permitted until a special Alaska Coal Leasing Act was passed by the Sixty-third Congress in 1914.

The effect of these federal land policies is clearly revealed by the pattern of land ownership that existed when the Alaska Statehood Law was enacted in 1958. In that year 99.8 percent of the land was still owned by the federal government. Only a little over a half million acres had passed into private ownership. Lands withdrawn and reserved by various federal agencies for permanent public ownership encompassed over 92 million acres, over a quarter of the total land area of the state, while the remaining area of about 270 million acres was vacant, unappropriated federal public domain lands under the jurisdiction of the Bureau of Land Management.[3] Details of this land ownership pattern for the years 1958 and 1963 are shown in Table 1. The distribution of land among the different agencies has varied, but the total amount of land in federal reserve status remained relatively constant until a short while ago, when there occurred two significant changes. In 1960, the Fish and Wildlife Service added over 11 million to its reserves in Alaska through creation by executive order of the Arctic National Wildlife Range in the northeastern corner of Alaska and the Izembek and Clarence Rhode waterfowl refuges in southwestern Alaska. In 1965 approximately another 9 million acres (not included in the table) were withdrawn from the public domain and reserved as a water-power site (P.S.O. 445) in contemplation of the proposed Rampart Dam power project on the Yukon River.[4] While some reserved lands have been returned to the public domain since 1964, these two withdrawals have resulted in an increase in federal reserved lands to over 100 million acres. The larger federal reserves are shown in Map 5.

The size and significance of these federal land holdings in

3. Responsibility for stewardship of the federal public domain evolved from an 1812 Congressional act establishing the General Land Office "to perform all actions and things touching or respecting the public lands of the United States." In 1946, the General Land Office was consolidated with the Grazing Service to form the Bureau of Land Management in the Department of the Interior which contains many other federal resource agencies including the National Park Service, the Fish and Wildlife Service, the Bureau of Outdoor Recreation, the Bureau of Reclamation, the Geological Survey, and the Bureau of Mines. Two other major federal resource agencies not included in the Interior Department are the Forest Service in the Department of Agriculture and the Corps of Engineers in the Department of the Army.

4. Lands classified as water power sites are open to location under mining and mineral leasing laws, and they may be entered under the public land laws with suitable provisions for the protection of power values following a favorable determination by the Federal Power Commission. In this respect, they are much less restrictive than other federal reserved lands.

TABLE 1
Land Status in Alaska

Status of Land	Acres	
	1958	1963
Federal Land Reserves		
National forests	20,700,000	20,700,000
Wildlife refuges and ranges (FWS)	7,800,000	19,000,000
Petroleum Reserve No. 4 (Navy)	23,000,000	23,000,000
National parks and monuments	6,900,000	6,900,000
Power reserves, etc. (BLM)	27,400,000	16,800,000 *
Indian reservations, school reserves, etc. (BIA)	4,100,000	4,100,000
Military reservations †	2,300,000	1,900,000
Other	200,000	200,000
Total reserves	92,400,000	92,600,000
Vacant, unappropriated public domain lands	271,800,000	259,200,000
Private ownership, patented and certified	700,000	900,000 ‡
Unperfected entries	600,000	12,800,000 §
Total Alaska land area	365,500,000	365,500,000

* 1958 includes 25 million acres in Northern Alaska Petroleum Reserve; the reserve was revoked in 1960 by a Public Land Order but 11.3 million acres were still not available for oil and gas leasing and so were included in the table as reserved.
† Includes Army, Navy, Air Force, and Corps of Engineers.
‡ Estimated on the basis of available data.
§ Includes state land selections of 12,400,000 acres pending approval for patent to state. (Total state selections amounted to 15,700,000 acres on Dec. 31, 1964.)
Source: 1958 data from General Services Administration, Washington, D.C.; 1963 data from U.S. Dept. of the Interior, *Public Land Statistics, 1963* (Washington: Govt. Printing Office, 1964), pp. 12–31.

Alaska becomes clearer when they are compared with federal land holdings in the nation as a whole. Today, nearly half of all land owned by the federal government is located in Alaska. The state contains 11 percent of all national forest reserves; 31 percent of all national park lands, 64 percent of all the remaining, vacant, unappropriated public domain and other lands under the exclusive jurisdiction of the Bureau of Land Management; 70 percent of all lands reserved by the Fish and Wildlife Service for wildlife ranges and refuges; and over 85 percent of all lands under the jurisdiction of the Bureau of Indian Affairs. These impressive figures reflect both the ease with which land could be reserved in Alaska for a multitude of government purposes and the high value placed upon certain of Alaska's lands and resources in the national interest.

The federal land policies became the root of an important and increasingly bitter political controversy in Alaska. Most of the federal land managing agencies were interested primarily in holding lands in Alaska for some undetermined future use. Seeing their role as a "custodial" one, they gave little consideration to planning for the future or to coordinating the programs of the many federal agencies. Their attitude was to a large extent conditioned by a lack of demand for the resources these lands could provide, but still many Alaskans came to regard conservationists as a group of unscrupulous politicians who were retarding the development and settlement of the north through overly restrictive and unworkable land laws and an overenthusiastic withdrawal and reservation of land. In a speech on the floor of the House of Representatives in 1911, Alaska's congressional delegate exclaimed:

> May the Congress, then, depart from republican principles in its legislation and establish a communist form of government in a Territory? May it establish a national coal land leasing monopoly, a national oil land leasing monopoly, a national fur-seal leasing monopoly, a national forest land monopoly, and a national monopoly of all the other resources of that helpless Territory, in its own right, as a national landlord, for national profit; and use the public domain . . . and the powers and instrumentalities of the Nation . . . for its exclusive national business enterprises? May it withdraw the public domain and its treasures from 'the people who own it' and reduce them to the status of tenants upon the estate of the national landlord? [5]

The first Alaska Territorial Legislature in 1913 transmitted to Congress a series of six memorials pleading that Land Office appropriations be increased for land surveys and improved administration in Alaska. It demanded that there be an end to federal reservations and "the land thrown open for the general

5. From *A National Coal Monopoly in Alaska*, reprint of a speech on the floor of the House of Representatives by the Honorable James Wickersham, Delegate for Alaska, February 23, 1911 (Washington: Govt. Printing Office, 1911), p. 33.

use of the prospector, miner and settler."[6] Each succeeding territorial legislature, and nearly every governor and territorial official, pressed for congressional action. Phrases like "putting Alaska in deep freeze" and "locking up Alaska resources" gained popular acceptance, as did the belief that the economy would immediately flourish if only "the shackles of the federal bureaucracy upon the land" could be thrown off. In the early 1940's the amount of land the federal government should grant to Alaska upon its entrance into the Union became a burning issue in the battle for statehood. Land grant provisions of the early statehood bills introduced in Congress ranged from 21 million acres to over 300 million acres, the minimum representing the amount of land Alaska would receive if Congress chose to follow the traditional practice of granting newly created states two sections out of each township for the support of schools, and the maximum including the national forests and other significant federal reserved lands. But by the time the Alaska Statehood Act was finally passed on July 7, 1958, land grant provisions had been hammered out which avoided these earlier extremes and expressed a rational balance between the economic needs of the new state and the important national interest existing in its lands and resources.

Under provisions of the Statehood Act, Alaska was given a period of twenty-five years to select 102,550,000 acres from the "vacant, unappropriated and unreserved" federal public domain lands within its borders, to be used for the general support of the state. It was also permitted to select during the same period an additional 400,000 acres from the national forests and another 400,000 acres from the vacant public domain for the specific purposes of community expansion and recreational use. Minor grants for the support of schools (approximately 200,000 acres) and a mental health program (one million acres), resulting from legislation passed prior to the Statehood Act, brought the total amount of federal lands available to the state for selection to over 104 million acres. As shown in Figure 1, no other state has

6. House Joint Memorials Nos. 3, 4, 6, 7, and 15, and Senate Joint Resolution No. 6, First Alaska Territorial Legislature, 1913.

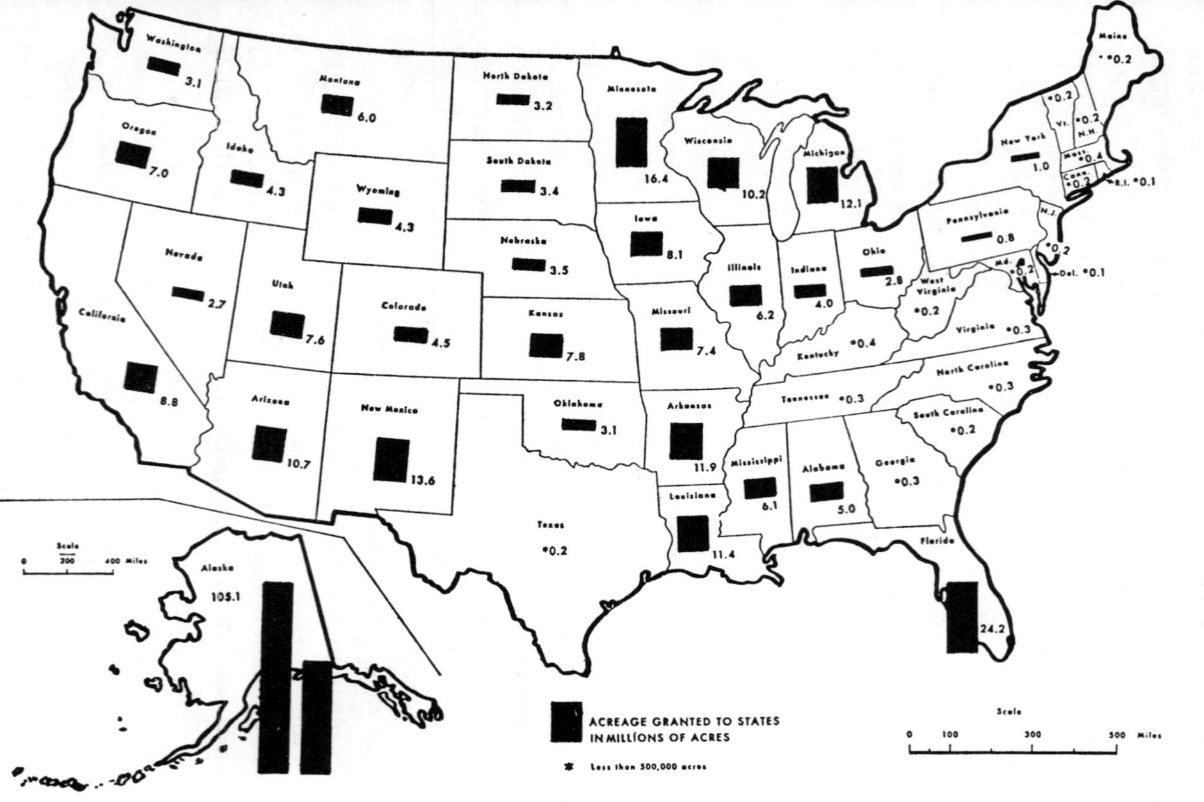

Figure 1: Federal Land Grants to States, 1803–1963

Source: U.S. Department of the Interior, *Public Land Statistics, 1963* (Washington: Govt. Printing Office, 1964), pp. 6–8.

received anywhere near as large a land grant. In fact, the grant to Alaska exceeds the total of all federal lands granted to the seventeen western states.

Statehood also brought other valuable lands under the state's jurisdiction. During the territorial period, the federal government held the tidelands "in trust" for the future state. These lands, lying between mean high and mean low tides, were not considered part of the public domain, and Congress did not allow them to be patented. They automatically became state property on January 1, 1959, under the equal footing clause of the United States Constitution which provides that all new states shall receive the same rights and privileges offered others. In addition, the Submerged Lands Act of 1953 (Public Law 83–31) stipulated that new states henceforth would receive title to all submerged lands lying three miles seaward of mean low tide, including the bottoms of historic bays and inland navigable waters. The ownership status of these lands was long a matter of controversy in the other states. Alaska thus became the first state to enter the Union with a free title to both its tidelands and submerged lands. Virtually none of these lands have been surveyed, and the irregular shape of Alaska's coastline makes it difficult to calculate their exact extent, but the state Division of Lands has estimated that from 35 to 45 million acres are involved.

Table 2 presents a summary of the land grants and other acreages comprising Alaska's potential land estate. If the state chooses to select all of the federal lands authorized by Congress, it will eventually become the owner of some 140 to 150 million acres, including tidal and submerged land.

The land grant provided in the Alaska Statehood Act clearly differs not only in its size but in its abandonment of the historic system of "in-place" land grants based on specified numbered sections within each township. It was widely recognized in congressional hearings and committee reports dealing with statehood that this anachronistic disposal method had resulted in a checkerboard pattern of land ownership in the western states that was not conducive to wise land management. Congress also

TABLE 2
Federal Land Grants to Alaska

Type of Grant	Acreage	Purpose and Source
Statehood grant lands	102,350,000	General purpose under authority of Statehood Act. (To be selected within 25 years)
Statehood grant lands	800,000	Community expansion and recreation in national forests and public domain. Authority of Statehood Act. (To be selected within 25 years)
Mental health lands	1,000,000	Support of mental health program. Selection authority granted to territory in 1956, and confirmed by Statehood Act. (To be selected within 10 years)
Tidelands and submerged lands	35,000,000–45,000,000	Federal government automatically transferred title with statehood. Lands are unsurveyed.
School lands	106,000	Support of public school system. Includes section 16 x 36 in every township if sections were surveyed prior to statehood (48 USCA 353, Mar. 4, 1915). Repealed by Statehood Act.
University quantity grant lands	100,000	Support of state university. Selection authority granted to territory in 1929. Confirmed by Statehood Act.
University Tanana Valley grant lands	9,504	Support of state university. Includes all surveyed section 33's in Tanana Valley (48 USCA 353, Mar. 4, 1915). Repealed by Statehood Act.
Public Law 507 lands	1,187	Improved recreation sites transferred to state by special legislation.
Alaska Omnibus Act lands	N.A.	Miscellaneous lands conveyed in 1959; mainly improved properties such as office buildings, maintenance buildings, etc. (All titles not yet processed to state)
Estimated total land grants	140,000,000–150,000,000	

Source: State of Alaska, Department of Natural Resources, Division of Lands.

realized that the new state could create a fiscally sound government only by heavy reliance upon the development of its lands and resources. So little of Alaska had been surveyed that grants of specified sections under the traditional formula would have made very little land immediately available; and in the long run as surveying progressed, the new state would have received title to large acreages of swamplands, mountain peaks, glaciers, tundra, and other lands of little foreseeable economic value. In addition, under the in-place system many of the specified numbered sections would have fallen within the large areas of federal reserved lands, and the selection of substitute lands would have been a complicated matter. The Alaska Statehood Act therefore nullified all of the earlier laws providing in-place land grants to new states for common schools, higher education, swampland reclamation, internal improvements, and other purposes, and substituted so-called quantity grants.

In many important ways the Statehood Act broke with past precedents. Alaska was given great freedom of choice in the selection of lands. Few limitations have been placed on the state's selection authority:

(1) All lands must be selected within 25 years from the date of Alaska's admission to the Union (i.e., by 1984).

(2) All selections must be made from the "vacant, unappropriated and unreserved public domain" (except for the 400,000 acres to be selected from the national forests).

(3) All selections must be made "in reasonably compact tracts . . . containing at least 5,760 acres, unless isolated from other tracts open to selections," (however, in the case of selections for purposes of community expansion and recreation, the minimum unit is 160 acres).

(4) All lands selected from the national forests and the public domain under the community expansion and recreation grant (i.e., 400,000 acres from each) must be "adjacent to established communities or suitable for prospective community centers," and must be approved, respectively, by the Secretary of Agriculture or the Secretary of the Interior.

(5) As a defense measure, all lands selected north of the Porcupine, Yukon, and Kuskokwim rivers must have the approval of the President of the United States.

Since there are well over 270 million acres of land open to selection under these broad terms, the state of Alaska was given an unprecedented opportunity to plan and carry out a realistic land selection program designed to meet its particular needs without undue federal interference, and indeed with some federal assistance. The federal government is for instance required to survey the exterior boundaries of each state selection prior to the issuance of patent, thus greatly reducing the direct costs of the land selection program to the state.

Another major departure from precedent concerns rights to minerals. The in-place grants received by the western states upon their entrance into the Union could not include mineral lands. If the specified sections were mineral in character, the state was forced to take others. In 1927, Congress changed this rule (44 U.S. Stat., 1026), to allow those states that had not yet taken all of their sections to take them even if they were known to contain minerals. The statute specified, however, that the states could never alienate their title to these minerals, but could only lease them. This important change in policy was carried over into the Alaska Statehood Act which expressly provides that all minerals in the lands selected are reserved to the state which may lease the deposits but cannot sell, grant, deed, or otherwise dispose of them. When any state land is sold, all mineral rights remain with the state. This clause should help reduce conflicts in the multiple use of lands; and the leasing technique, with its rentals and royalties and its performance and development clauses, should assure that permanent financial returns accrue to the state in the development of its mineral wealth. It does, however, create a duality of land systems with potential federal-state conflict since mineral lands can be brought to patent under federal law.

One other distinctive feature of the Alaska Statehood Act bears mentioning. Alaska receives a far larger share of federal revenues from the so-called leasable minerals (e.g. coal, oil, gas, phosphate, and sodium) on the public domain than does any other state. The western states, being considered reclamation states, receive directly only 37½ percent of the federal revenues, while another 52½ percent is paid into the reclamation fund.[7] Since Alaska has not been classified as a reclamation state, Congress provided that the entire 90 percent should go to the state government, including receipts from rentals, royalties, and bonuses. No other state enjoys this large and continuing source of revenue from federal lands.

An examination of these land provisions in the Alaska Statehood Act makes it clear that Congress was attempting to accomplish two ends. One was to avoid past mistakes in congressional policy which had resulted in unsatisfactory patterns of land ownership and land use in the western states. The other was to provide the state of Alaska with ample authority to select the lands and resources necessary to the development of a broad economic base capable of supporting a fiscally sound state government, yet in so doing, not to neglect the national interest. Congress has indeed been generous with Alaska.

7. The reclamation fund was set up by the Reclamation Act of 1902. According to the act, all money received from sale and disposal of public lands in reclamation states (i.e., Arizona, California, Colorado, Idaho, Kansas, Montana, Nebraska, Nevada, New Mexico, North Dakota, Oklahoma, Oregon, South Dakota, Utah, Washington, and Wyoming) are set aside as a special fund to be used for irrigation and reclamation works.

Chapter 3

A New Policy for Land Use

ALASKA'S first few years of statehood have seen impressive accomplishments in three important areas of land policy. A constitutional framework has been provided, the state legislature has drawn up a land and resource code, and implementation of the constitutional and statutory provisions has begun.

The Alaska State Constitution was adopted by the people in 1956, two years before passage of the Statehood Act. For most states, constitutions were written before the growth of public awareness of the importance of land and resource policy. The delegates to the Alaskan convention, however, were presented with an opportunity to draft a policy for the use and conservation of natural resources on a scale and with a purpose no other state had envisioned, and they were also aware that the quality of the constitution they produced would largely determine whether Congress would pass a statehood bill. With this additional inducement to create a document soundly conceived in all its parts, they designed in Article VIII an excellently drawn set of provisions for natural resources. The Alaska constitution is one of the first state constitutions to include a general statement of policy on the use, disposition, and conservation of all land and other natural resources.

The natural resources article sets out the broad policy of the state "to encourage the settlement of its lands and the development of its resources by making them available for maximum use consistent with the public interest." Free access to the public waters of the state cannot be denied any citizen except as may be necessary to protect the public interest; and surface uses of land by a mineral claimant are limited to those necessary for the extraction and basic processing of mineral deposits. The legislature is specifically empowered to withdraw and reserve lands from the state public domain that are important for their natural beauty, or are of historical, cultural, scientific, or recreational value, and to "provide for their administration and preservation for the use, enjoyment and welfare of the people."

All replenishable natural resources belonging to the state, including fish, forests, wildlife, and grasslands must be developed and maintained "on the sustained yield principle, subject to preferences among beneficial users." This latter section is one of the most important, for it represents a direct mandate to the state government to manage all of its renewable natural resources on a scientific basis, paying close attention to modern principles of multiple use and sustained yield management. The state cannot sell, grant, or deed its rights to these renewable natural resources, but can only lease them with proper precautions for their conservation. It is the first provision of this type ever to be written into a state constitution, and it should help avert the destructive exploitation of resources that earlier occurred on the lands of many western states.

Equally important from the aspect of good constitutional law, all policy decisions to implement these general aims were left to the discretion of the legislature. There is no attempt either to dilute the responsibility of the legislature for establishing a resource code or to dictate its administrative machinery and the offices to be established. The writing of such administrative details into state constitutions—as occurred in many western states—was generally the result of efforts to take land and resource administration "out of politics," but frequently led to more—not less—politics besides making it much more difficult to coordinate resource programs with other activities of state government. In the Alaska constitution, the legislature is given clear-cut authority to "provide for the utilization, development, and conservation of all natural resources belonging to the state, including land and waters, for the maximum benefit of its people." All lands acquired by the state, including submerged and tidal lands, constitute the state public domain, and the legislature is authorized to set up the machinery required to select, manage, and dispose of state lands, and to establish policies and procedures for the lease, sale, or grant of state-owned lands within the broad dictates of the constitution. All laws and regulations must apply equally to all persons, and no disposal of state lands can be made without prior public notice and other procedural safeguards to protect the public interest. The legislature is also authorized to make provisions for the issuance of permits for the private exploration and development of the public domain under government regulation, and to provide government facilities, improvements, and services to induce greater use, development, reclamation, and settlement of lands and resources.

In 1959, the first session of the First Alaska State Legislature enacted three laws having special significance for the state land program. The basic organization of the executive branch of government was provided for in the State Organization Act (64 SLA 1959), which established twelve separate departments with full executive authority and responsibility concentrated in the governor. A Department of Natural Resources was created and vested with the administration of the entire program for the conservation and development of the state's natural resources, including lands, water, forests, agriculture, soils, recreation, and minerals; only fish and game resources were placed in a separate department. The act carried through the constitutional concept of a strong executive by giving the governor wide discretionary powers in determining the internal organization of the separate departments. He appoints all department heads, the only two elective positions in the entire executive branch being his own and that of the Secretary of State. This streamlined form of government organization, with its clear lines of accountability running through the governor to the people, has been instrumental in the development of an efficient and responsive state land program.

The Alaska Land Act (169 SLA 1959) established the Division of Lands within the Department of Natural Resources as the organization to select, manage, and dispose of state lands. The functions of the Division also include the management and protection of state forest lands; the planning, development, and maintenance of a state parks and recreation system; the leasing of minerals (including oil and gas); and the encouragement of mining developments on state lands. Figure 2 shows the functional organization of the Division as it is now constituted, with five separate branches.

The Land Act provides basic policy guidelines for land management. The most significant highlights are: the authority to classify lands to their highest and best use on the basis of area land-use plans; limitations on the disposal of certain classes of lands in the public interest; requirements for the competitive lease and sale of lands suitable for disposal; provisions for the multiple use of state lands; and responsiveness to public desires through an established procedure of public hearings on all rule making, including the classification and reclassification of lands. This last provision has been reinforced by provisions in the Administrative Procedures Act (143 SLA 1959), which requires that all regulations promulgated by the Division must be subjected to public hearings before they become effective. The act insures that people will be given adequate notice of impending administrative changes, and it provides an effective means for land management officials to capitalize on the experience, knowledge, and interests of the citizenry in deciding policies and procedures. It has in effect given people a feeling of participation in the governmental process—a frame of mind that was absent during territorial days. All the above acts were given greater effectiveness by the establishment of a civil service system which has helped attract competent personnel to administer the Land Act.

Shortly after its formation in 1959, the Division of Lands launched a long series of public hearings throughout the state to

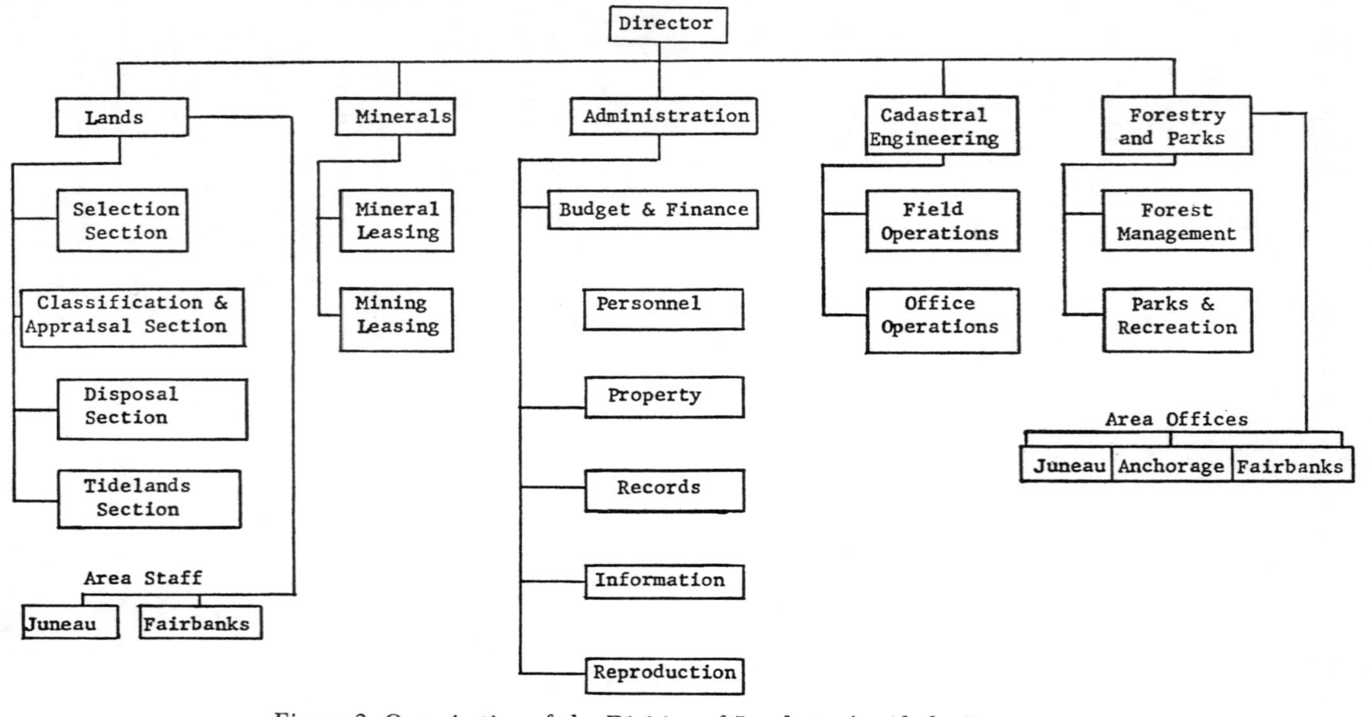

Figure 2: Organization of the Division of Lands in the Alaska Department of Natural Resources

design and formulate regulatory policies and procedures within the framework of the constitution and the Land Act. Detailed regulations now have been established governing land classification, the lease and sale of lands, homesteading, the sale of timber, minerals, and other materials, oil and gas leasing, and tideland leasing. A concise review of these offers a perspective of the scope and direction of the state land program.[1]

The main management tool provided in the Alaska Land Act is the authority to classify lands to their highest and best use. In its regulations, the Division of Lands has defined this to mean that all state lands must be classified prior to any disposal action. Area land-use plans must first be prepared and approved by the Commissioner of Natural Resources, and the classification of specific tracts within each area is based upon these plans. Climate, soils, vegetation, and other physical, economic, and social criteria are taken into consideration in preparing the plans and in determining particular land classifications. When the land is within or adjacent to communities or settled areas, the proposed land-use plans must be submitted to local planning agencies or to citizens' groups for review. This reduces the likelihood of arbitrary actions by state officials and has encouraged cooperative state and local planning for the use of lands and resources within these areas.

How the land is classified determines whether the Division can make it available for sale or lease, and whether it must be retained permanently in state ownership in accordance with the constitutional provisions mentioned earlier. There are thirteen different classifications under present regulations:

LANDS RETAINED PERMANENTLY IN STATE OWNERSHIP

Mineral Lands

Lands that are chiefly valuable for minerals, including but not limited to coal, phosphate, oil shale, sodium, sulphur, and potash,

1. The Division of Lands regulations are published in State of Alaska, Administrative Code, Title II (Natural Resources), Division I (Lands) (mimeo). The following discussion of land regulations is taken from this source.

and where the removal of the mineral would seriously interfere with surface rights. Mineral removal is allowed by lease or staked claim in accordance with Division regulations. The land may also be leased for purposes other than the removal of minerals if consistent with the public interest.

Material Lands

Lands chiefly valuable for materials, including but not limited to sand, gravel, stone, pumice, cinders, and clay, and where the removal of the materials would seriously interfere with surface utilization. Materials may be purchased and removed in accordance with Division regulations. The land may also be leased for purposes other than the removal of material if consistent with the basic purpose.

Timber Lands

Lands which, because of physical, climatic, and vegetative conditions are presently or potentially valuable chiefly for the production of timber and other forest products. The timber may be purchased and removed in accordance with Division regulations under a sustained yield program. The land may also be leased for other purposes when consistent with multiple use management of forest lands.

Grazing Lands

Lands having physical and climatic features that make them primarily useful for the pasturing of domestic livestock. For lease only.

Public Recreation Lands

Lands which may be utilized best by the public for parks, scenic overlooks, campgrounds, historic sites, hunting and fishing access sites, etc. They may be leased for other purposes provided the contemplated use is consistent with the primary purpose. Leases are subject to such restrictions as are deemed necessary to protect public recreational use.

Watershed Lands

Lands encompassing a drainage area which can best be utilized as a public water source. They may be leased only for purposes consistent with the public interest in accordance with Division regulations.

Reserved Use Lands

Lands designated for present or future public use, for the use of government agencies, or for the development of townsites. They may be disposed of only to a government or quasi-government agency.

LANDS AVAILABLE FOR DISPOSAL (SALE OR LEASE)

Agricultural Lands

Lands having physical, climatic, and economic features that make them suitable primarily for the production of agricultural crops. The land may be disposed of by lease, sale, or homesteading.

Commercial Lands

Lands which because of location, physical features, or adjacent developments, can best be utilized for commercial purposes. The land may be disposed of by lease or sale.

Industrial Lands

Lands which because of location, physical features, or adjacent developments, can be utilized for industrial purposes. The land may be disposed of by lease or sale.

Private Recreation Lands

Lands which are chiefly valuable as outdoor rural areas and may best be utilized for private noncommercial development such as summer cabins, camps, etc. The land may be disposed of by lease or sale.

Residential Lands

Lands which, because of location, physical features, or adjacent development, may best be utilized for single or multiple unit dwellings. The land may be disposed of by lease or sale.

Utility Lands

Lands which may be suitable for a variety of uses but which do not lend themselves to classification under the other designations. The land may be disposed of by lease or sale for any purpose.

All land transferred to the state's jurisdiction is in an unclassified status. No disposal of lands or resources is permitted until the land has been inventoried and classified in one of these thirteen categories, the only exception being that the leasing and claim-staking of minerals is allowed on unclassified land. The regulations contain a provision permitting reclassification of lands when necessary, thus giving the state sufficient flexibility to take account of shifts in development, population, new industries, and other changes that may influence the demand for particular classes of land. And in all cases the Division may permit multiple use of classified lands provided such uses are compatible with the purpose of the primary classification.

The state can exercise significant controls over mining activities on certain important classes of lands. Agricultural, commercial, industrial, private recreation, public recreation, residential, watershed, and reserved-use lands are closed to the removal of minerals except upon the issuance of a mining lease or permit of such removal. If it is deemed in the public interest, the Division of Lands may reject a mineral lease applicant, or may place restrictions in the lease to insure that the mining operation is conducted in a manner that will not conflict unduly with the use for which the land was classified.

The classification authority is, in effect, an important zoning implement that places the state in a favorable position to encourage the orderly development of state lands and resources. In seven out of the thirteen classifications, the land itself is retained permanently in public ownership. Timber lands, mineral lands, material lands, public recreation lands, grazing lands, watershed lands, and reserved-use lands cannot be sold. They may be leased, or the resources may be sold from them, but only in accordance with stipulated government regulations to protect the public interest. And the state can control the pattern of private development and settlement of its lands by determining when, where, and how much land will be placed on the market at any given time for sale or lease in the other six classifications (i.e. agricultural, commercial, industrial, private recreation, residential, and utility lands). No land can be sold by the Division unless it has first been classified in one of these categories, and these lands are not open to entry in the sense that the phrase is generally used; it is, rather, the prerogative of the director of the Division of Lands to determine which lands will be placed on the market, and when, and to stipulate the conditions or limitations that may attach to the lands to be sold. All lands must first be offered for sale at a public auction after adequate public notice has been given. The minimum acceptable price is the fair market value as determined by qualified land appraisers on the Division's staff, and no land can be sold unless it was appraised at least ninety days before the sale. The land goes to the highest bidder; land not sold at the public auction is available thereafter for purchase at the fair market value on a "first come–first served" basis and may be paid for in annual installments over a ten-year period at an interest rate of five percent. No individual or corporation may purchase more than 640 acres of state land except under special conditions.

All of these procedural safeguards also pertain to the leasing of state lands and resources. Leases are issued for any period up to fifty-five years, with the annual rental payments subject to adjustment every five years. The Division may impose restrictions and reservations to protect the interests of the state, may require the submission of a development plan for all leases of over 640 acres, and can cancel the lease for failure to make substantial use of the land in keeping with the plan. Leases are awarded at public auction after due advertising, and leases not issued at the auction are available for purchase at any time on a fair market rental basis.

The sale of timber from state lands is also conducted at competitive sales, either by the submission of written sealed bids or by public outcry auctions.[2] The first section in the timber sales regulations declares that "it is the policy of the State of Alaska to manage its timber lands for the maximum benefit of the people, consistent with the professional concepts of multiple-use and sustained yield as recognized and practiced by the forestry profession." Timber sale contracts contain detailed provisions regarding logging methods, silvicultural practices, reforestation, fire prevention, protection of watershed and recreational values, etc. The state can, in fact, regulate virtually all aspects of the timber enterprise to prevent damage to other resources, protect streams, reduce hazards, control road construction, and otherwise assure the conduct of sound and orderly operations. The sale of other materials is carried out under somewhat similar stipulations although the Division can negotiate a sale without competitive bidding if the value of the materials is less than $2,500.

As was already mentioned, the federal Homestead Act was originally designed to meet the needs of the western states, and neither the provision which set the size of individual units at 160 acres nor the requirements for residency and cultivation were suited to the conditions existing in Alaska. Although much of the land that passed from federal to private ownership in Alaska during territorial days had been transferred under this act, very little permanent agricultural development actually occurred.[3] The state, recognizing these inadequacies, has attempted to develop homestead regulations tailored to the particular physical, eco-

2. Noncompetitive sales may be made when it is determined to be in the best interests of the state. However, such sales are limited to a volume of 500,000 board feet.

3. For a detailed analysis of this problem see Hugh A. Johnson and Robert Coffman, *Land Occupancy, Ownership and Use on Homesteads in the Kenai Peninsula, Alaska, 1955,* Alaska Agricultural Experiment Station, Bul. 21, Nov. 1956.

nomic, and social conditions of Alaska. Two specifications must be met before state lands can be homesteaded. First, the land must be classified as suitable for the production of agricultural crops; and second, it must be declared available for homesteading by the Division of Lands. By judicious use of these powers, the Division can control homesteading in the best interests of the state's development. It can for instance insure that it takes place only in relatively compact areas where public services already exist, or where they can be provided without undue cost to the state. Those lands designated as available for homesteading are sold at public auction to the highest bidder, under the same procedures as other state lands. The appraised fair market value is the minimum price the state will accept, and payments may be extended over a ten-year period. The state, unlike the federal program, does not require a period of residency or the cultivation of a definite acreage before purchase. An individual may homestead or patent up to 640 acres, or four times the maximum acreage allowed on the federal public domain under the Homestead Act.

A unique feature of the state homestead program is a system of "improvement credits" designed to assist and encourage the genuine settler who actually intends to farm the land. Instead of using his limited capital to purchase the land, the homesteader may write off all or part of the remaining land costs after the initial down payment by making improvements which will enhance the value of the land. Improvement costs that may be charged off against the purchase price include land clearing and drainage, fencing, well drilling, access roads, construction of family dwellings or farm buildings, and other approved developments according to a set schedule laid out in the regulations. It is a flexible incentive program that gives the individual purchaser wide latitude in determining when and how much to invest in development of the land in accordance with his own particular financial situation.

Since Congress stipulated that all mineral rights were reserved to the state, it was necessary for the Division of Lands to take an entirely fresh approach in devising provisions to regulate the discovery and removal of minerals from the state public domain. Under federal laws, mineral claims on federal lands can be patented, and title to the land passes into private ownership. This system has been well regarded generally by private mining interests since it gives them great freedom in the exploration and development of mining deposits discovered on federal lands. The system has however inhibited the multiple use of the nation's resources, and resource managers now widely recognize that the general mining laws of the United States need to be revised to meet modern day conditions. It is possible that the innovations contained in the Alaska Land Law, and the subsequent regulatory policies issued by the Division, forecast the direction and scope of future change in national policy.

All state lands are open to mineral exploration. Since the state retains mineral rights when the land is sold, exploration can also occur on state lands that have passed into private ownership. Once a valid discovery is made, the minerals can be mined and removed under a leasing arrangement or by staking a mining claim location. The latter can be staked only on unclassified land or on lands whose primary use would not be unduly damaged or interfered with by the mining operation (i.e., lands classified as grazing, timber, material, and mineral lands). In all other classifications, actual mining cannot take place until a lease has been issued, and if the Division of Lands determines that the mining development conflicts with the primary values for which the land was classified, the director may deny the lease or make stipulations and limitations to protect the public interest. In areas where vegetation, depth of overburden or other physical conditions make prospecting exceptionally difficult and costly, a system of prospecting permits [4] has been devised to provide protection and inducement to prospectors. By agreeing to conduct a prospecting program of a specified magnitude using modern techniques, a locator of a site can obtain exclusive pre-discovery rights to all

4. Prospecting permits are issued for coal and other Leasing Act minerals but not for the so-called locatable minerals such as the precious and base metals.

minerals found within a limited area. The permits are for one year but may be extended.

The leasing of coal, oil, gas, phosphates, sodium, sulphur, and potassium deposits on state lands is covered by rules and regulations modeled after the federal policies for the so-called leasable minerals as provided in the Mineral Leasing Act of 1920 (41 U.S. Stat., 437). The Division has given greatest emphasis to perfecting regulations for the leasing of oil and gas, since these resources offered the most immediate possibilities for development.

Oil and gas leases are of two types. Competitive leases are required for lands within a known geological structure of a producing oil and gas field; for tidal and submerged lands; and for lands that were granted to the state specifically for the support of the University and the mental health program.[5] They are issued at auction to the qualified bidder who submits the highest offer as a "bonus" for the privilege of obtaining the lease for a ten-year period. Noncompetitive leases are required for all other state lands and are issued to the first qualified applicant making an offer. These leases are for a five-year period but may be renewed under certain specified conditions. An annual rental is charged for each competitive or noncompetitive lease, and a royalty of 12½ percent must be paid to the state when production begins. The state has authority to prevent companies from holding oil and gas in reserve if a market exists, and in the interest of conservation it can regulate every aspect of the drilling and operation of oil and gas wells on all lands, whether state, federal, or private.[6]

State regulations for leasable minerals are less restrictive in a number of respects than federal policies. Under the state program, a lessee may hold a maximum of 500,000 acres, or one million acres on tide and submerged lands, while on federal lands the maximum is only 300,000 acres.[7] State regulations contain a

5. The state has other powers to classify lands for competitive oil and gas leasing, and in this respect has much broader authority than the federal government.

6. Oil and Gas Conservation Act (Ch. 40 SLA 1955, as amended by Ch. 75 SLA 1960).

7. Actually, however, under federal regulations a lessee may hold 300,000 acres in each of two leasing districts in Alaska.

special "discovery incentive," not provided under federal law, which entitles a person who drills and makes the first discovery of oil and gas in commercial quantities to pay a reduced royalty on production from the discovery lease during the first ten years. The Division is also authorized to offer further incentives in granting permits for exploration and development when they are determined necessary to promote development and are in the interest of conservation. Companies may be permitted or required to enter into cooperative operating agreements if it is considered advisable to conserve the resource.

One of the most important and immediate tasks facing the state was to provide for the administration of the enormous tide and submerged lands which came under its jurisdiction. The Alaska Land Act of 1959 stipulated that the state would provide a patent to those persons who had developed and improved the tidelands prior to statehood, and that each coastal city incorporated before statehood could receive title to tidelands seaward of its boundaries. No other tide or submerged lands could be sold or granted away by the state; they could only be leased for a maximum period of fifty-five years. The intent of the act is to maintain as much of the tidelands as possible "open for the use and enjoyment of the public." Regulations to carry out the law were drafted and approved early in 1960, and since few coastal states have developed adequate regulations for their tidelands, these are primarily a product of the state itself.

When leased for purposes other than for oil and gas or minerals, tide and submerged lands first must be classified for the highest and best use and their fair market value determined. Tideland classifications generally conform to the thirteen upland categories where pertinent, and in nearly all cases are dictated primarily by the use or classification of the abutting uplands. Except in the case of oil and gas, the state does not offer tideland leases on its own initiative as it does for the uplands, but leaves it to the individual to make application to the state for the leasing of these lands. If the lease is for more than five years, or the annual rental charge exceeds $250, it must be advertised and offered at a public auction. Owners of coastal lands do not obtain first claim to lease the tidelands abutting their property, but they cannot be deprived of their right of access; and since the basic policy of state tideland leasing is to complement and facilitate upland use, it is unlikely that tidelands in front of an upland owner would be leased to a third party if the upland owner can demonstrate that the lease would jeopardize the use and enjoyment of his land.[8] Special regulations were also adopted to permit the equitable leasing of shore space for fishery developments, such as the leasing of set net sites in connection with the salmon fishery.[9]

These are the basic tools devised by the state of Alaska to carry out its responsibilities for the selection, management, and disposal of its lands. They provide a highly flexible framework of regulations giving the Division of Lands wide latitude in determining objectives and in setting priorities for the multiple use of state lands. At the same time, however, there are safeguards to insure that the program is carried out in accordance with modern principles of land management. The regulations spell out the *modus operandi* of land administration in Alaska. Continual revision is occurring as the need for changes becomes apparent, and each year new hearings are held to devise procedures for other important but less urgent areas of land policy.

8. Kirk W. Stanley, "Alaska Tidelands, Their Uses and Development," reprint from *Shore and Beach,* Oct. 1962. This article contains a very good review of the state program for tide and submerged lands by the state official in charge.

9. The Shore Fishery Leasing Regulations were promulgated under special enabling legislation passed in 1963 (Ch. 93 SLA 1963). This is a complex and controversial subject, and the residents of at least one coastal area (Yakutat) have gone on record as being strongly opposed to the leasing of fishery locations in their area.

Chapter 4

Land Office Business

THE laws and regulations fix the guidelines and etch the profile of the state land program, but the details of its operation and the rate of accomplishment are shaped by many different forces. Important among these is the way the state defines specific objectives and sets priorities. The Division of Lands has enunciated three major aims, presumably in the order of their importance:

To further economic development by making lands, minerals, timber, gravel, and other materials available for private development, and by working with individuals and existing or potential industries to assure maximum sustained use of resources.

To furnish state revenues by providing a solid base of recurring revenue from leases and sale contracts, by producing immediate revenue through competitive oil and gas lease sales, and by reducing state expenses through the furnishing of gravel and other materials, building sites, and rights-of-way for state and local governmental use.

To provide for the future by working to build a lasting foundation of resource availability and revenue production, by assuring that public park and recreational resources are conserved for the future, and by assisting and encouraging an orderly pattern of private and public development through informed land planning in cooperation with local communities and governmental bodies.[1]

By the end of 1965, the Division had selected nearly 17 million acres from the open federal public domain, an area larger than West Virginia. This represents about 15 percent of the total land grant, or an average of about 2.6 million acres per year. If the state is to claim all of the land available to it under the land grant provisions, the annual rate of selection will have to be increased and maintained at an average of about 5 million acres until the year 1984. To give an idea of the size of the job ahead, at this rate the state would have to select an area about the size of Rhode Island every sixty days during the next twenty years. Map 6 shows the general location of the selected lands, a large percentage of which is close to the bigger towns and cities. A wide time lag exists between the actual selection of lands by the state and the issuance of patent by the federal government; of the lands selected so far, the state has received tentative approval for a little over 10.5 million acres, while lands actually patented to the state amount to only about 2.5 million acres.

During the early years of the program the state and the Bureau of Land Management disagreed radically over the size of the basic selection unit, a matter having considerable economic importance since the federal agency is required by the Statehood Act to survey the exterior boundaries of each unit selected. By making a large number of small selections, the state could shift the greater part of the high costs of land surveying in Alaska to the Bureau. A distinct polarity of viewpoints developed between the two levels of government on the issue. On the one hand, the Bureau of Land Management contended that a provision in Section 6 of the Statehood Act which stated that selections should be "in reasonably compact tracts, taking into consideration the situation and the potential use of the lands involved" was the primary criterion to be used by the state; and following this line

1. Alaska Department of Natural Resources, Division of Lands, *Annual Report*, 1963, p. 1. (All statistics used in this chapter concerning state lands were obtained from the Division's monthly and annual reports; the figures have been rounded.)

of reasoning the federal agency in a number of cases demanded that the state select areas in excess of one million acres in order to form a "compact" unit. On the other hand, the state, relying primarily on another stipulation in the same section of the act—to the effect that each selection shall contain at least 5,760 acres—contended that a large compact land area could be taken up through a series of small selection units of this minimum size, and that the federal government was required by law to survey the boundaries of each. Federal action on a large number of state selections was withheld pending resolution of the conflict, and patenting of titles was very slow.

At a conference between state and federal officials in the summer of 1963, it was agreed that the state could select land by township units, each containing 23,040 acres, and that the federal agency would conduct surveys on this basis. Actually the state can still select in quarter-township size tracts if it prefers, but under the agreement the Bureau of Land Management will provide exterior boundary surveys on a township basis only. While this represented a compromise, still it placed on the federal government the principal financial burden of establishing a land survey network in Alaska, a cost that is exceptionally high because of the lack of earlier surveys, the physical characteristics of the terrain, and the extent of the job to be done. It also gave the state a much wider degree of latitude in land selections than would have been the case had the federal "compactness rule" dominated. It should be noted, however, that the state still has an extremely large surveying job ahead, because the land selections must be subdivided into small parcels by the state prior to any disposal action. (By contrast, most other states had their land grants completely surveyed by the federal government down to a quarter section, or 160 acres.) As a result, surveying continues to represent one of the major costs of land disposal to the state, though many new methods and techniques, such as the use of radar and helicopters, are being developed each year in an effort to lower these costs.

Since the 1963 agreement between the state and the Bureau of

Land Management, there has been a sharp rise in the amount of land tentatively approved by the federal agency (as may be seen in Table G in the appendix tables). There has also been an increase in the flow of land title to the state, though this has been less dramatic owing to the time required by the federal agency to clear title and survey the exterior boundaries before issuing patent. As a result of the agreement, however, it is expected that the time lag between selection and patent will be greatly reduced in the years ahead.

Of the 2.5 million acres of land patented to the state, nearly 400,000 acres have been classified to the highest and best use in accordance with state regulations. By the end of 1965 nearly 70,000 acres had been sold and some 125,000 were under lease for various private uses (excluding leases for oil and gas, minerals, and other materials, which are discussed later). A number of relatively large agricultural and utility tracts have been sold or leased, but most of this land has been disposed in small lots classified for residential, commercial, and private recreational uses in areas readily accessible to the main population centers. The demand for land in these latter classes and locations continues to exceed the supply, for although the Division has sought to place a sufficient number of these lots on sale at each auction to prevent overly inflated land values, the majority has invariably sold at well above the appraised market value. In some of the choicest locations near the larger communities, lands for private residential and recreational uses are bringing as much as $8,000 an acre at the state auctions. These high purchase prices also have resulted at least partially from a certain amount of speculative buying induced by the credit payment system which allows the purchaser to pay for the land over a ten-year period. Approximately 90 percent of all purchases have been on this basis.

Land not sold at public auction can be purchased over the counter in the Division's office at the appraised price. Since the inception of the program the Division has attempted to build a backlog of lands available for purchase in different parts of Alaska, but it has been difficult to stay abreast of current demands. A similar situation exists with lands available for leasing. As a result, by the end of 1965 the Division had less than 10,000 acres available over the counter for either sale or lease throughout the state.[2] Additional lands were being classified, appraised, surveyed, and placed on the market as rapidly as possible.

The state has also classified and placed on auction a total of 166 homestead units ranging up to 640 acres in size. Over three-quarters of these were sold at the auctions or immediately thereafter, nearly all of them at prices well above the minimum appraised value. So far, however, there has been very little actual farm development on these lands. The 1964 *Annual Report* of the Division of Lands showed, for example, that only one out of 129 homesteaders had applied for credit allowances that reduce the cost of the land to them if they make certain basic improvements on the property. The failure to use this credit allowance program is a good indication that homestead lands are being taken up for speculation or for uses other than farming, contrary to the intent of the law, just as was the case under the federal homestead program. An act passed in the 1965 State Legislature (97 SLA 1965) giving an established farmer a preference right to purchase or lease state agricultural lands "adjacent to or in close proximity of his presently held land," has created an additional problem. The intent of the law was to give the legitimate farmer an opportunity to purchase the land at a reasonable price for expansion of his agricultural enterprise in preference to the speculator who very likely would pay more for the land but would subdivide it for other more profitable nonagricultural uses. But however honorable the intent of the act, there are no safeguards to prevent the farmer himself from purchasing such lands with these other nonagricultural endeavors in mind, and so

2. Land for sale late in 1965 included 110 residential lots, 27 commercial lots, 25 recreational lots, 39 homestead units, 2 agricultural tracts, and 9 utility or miscellaneous tracts. Land for lease included 216 recreation lots, 19 commercial lots, and 1 agricultural tract. Source: Alaska Department of Natural Resources, Division of Lands, "Alaska Land Lines" (report for October, 1965).

the practical effect of the act has been to give the farmer a preference to speculate. Such ill-conceived class legislation should not be allowed to erode the state land program.

In spite of the high prices being paid for individual lots and tracts, the direct revenues from the lease and sale of state lands (not including oil and gas leases) have been small, averaging less than half a million dollars a year. This annual income, however, amounts to only a fraction of the total amount due the state in the future. The actual face value of land under active lease and sale contracts presently exceeds $5 million, and the revenue the state is now receiving merely represents the annual interest and installment payments on that amount. Each year as more lands are made available for lease and sale, the state can expect a steady increase in these recurring revenues. But more importantly, by making land available as rapidly as possible when and where it is in greatest demand, the Division is fulfilling one of its principal aims of promoting the economic development of the state. One example is particularly noteworthy. In 1961, the Standard Oil Company wanted to build an oil refinery on the Kenai Peninsula but no adequate private or federal lands were available for purchase along the coast in the right place. By special action, the Division selected a suitable tract and immediately made it available to the company. The sale resulted in a gain of $250,000 in state receipts and the refinery itself, which began operation in 1963, is a valuable addition to Alaska's economy. It takes time to develop an orderly land disposal program, but it is increasingly clear that the state program is beginning to meet many important needs which have in the past gone unfulfilled.

One of the activities most vital to economic advance and to the production of revenues has been the leasing of state lands for oil and gas exploration and development. At the time of the passage of the Statehood Act, the oil industry had already made a number of encouraging discoveries in Alaska on federal lands. Recognizing the revenue possibilities, the state immediately began to select those lands with the highest potential for the discovery of oil and gas, and took steps to lease it as rapidly as possible. Subsequent regulations, developed with the direct aim of encouraging and speeding oil and gas exploration and development on state lands, have produced outstanding results. By the end of 1965, the Division had conducted fifteen competitive lease sales which resulted in the leasing of over two million acres of state land (including tide and submerged lands), and had issued nearly one million acres of noncompetitive oil and gas leases. Cash bonuses paid to the state by the major oil companies as a result of the auctioning of competitive leases have amounted to approximately $65 million since statehood. The largest bonuses in any single year occurred in 1961 when four competitive lease sales resulted in over $22 million in direct revenues. The state also receives an annual rental from these leases amounting to about $2 million, and the production of oil and gas which commenced in 1964 now brings in another $2 million to the treasury each year. Though smaller, these rentals and royalties are much steadier sources of income in comparison with bonus payments which may fluctuate widely from year to year, and since prospects are bright for the continued growth of the industry, it may be expected that these recurring revenues will become relatively more important during the next few years.[3]

During the first seven years of statehood, total revenues from all state land transactions have amounted to about $70 million, or around 20 percent of all revenues paid into the state general fund. (Not included here are revenues from university, school, and mental health lands amounting to over $2½ million. These lands are administered by the Division but the income goes into special funds for these purposes.) Over 90 percent has come from oil and gas leasing, with the largest single source being the bonuses paid by major oil companies for competitive leases. A comparison of the annual operating costs of the Division with total revenues produced shows approximately a tenfold return on the invest-

3. See the Appendix Tables (Tables A and I) for figures on present royalties from oil and gas production with projections to 1970.

ment.[4] Other important land revenues accrue to the state general fund as a result of the stipulation in the Statehood Act giving Alaska 90 percent of all rentals and royalties received from federal mineral leasing activities. Under this provision the state enjoys the revenue without having to select and manage lands which may have no other long-term values warranting their inclusion in the state's permanent land estate. Payments to the state from this source alone have exceeded $40 million during the seven-year period, nearly all attributed to oil and gas activities. This sum has been augmented by approximately $5 million received in shared revenues from other federal programs involving land and resources, including 25 percent of the national forest timber sales receipts and 70 percent of the net proceeds from the annual sales of the Pribilof Island fur seal skins. Altogether, these various sources of revenue from state and federal lands have produced an income of over $115 million during the seven-year period, or approximately 30 percent of all receipts paid into the state general fund. Clearly, the new state government would have found it extremely difficult—if not impossible—to meet the growing costs of government during this critical transitional period without these important sources of revenue from the land.

The Division has embarked upon a number of significant programs where the emphasis is not upon immediate economic development or the production of larger current revenues. A program of forest management was launched early in 1959. Very little is known about the quality and quantity of the vast forests available for selèction in interior and southcentral Alaska, and the Division has sought above all to gain the knowledge required for rational decisions about the acquisition and development of a viable system of state forests. They have conducted both extensive and intensive inventories, with federal cooperation, to delineate forest management units for state selection, and have prepared timber management plans for the orderly sale of timber to

4. See the Statistical Appendix (Tables C and D) for a detailed presentation of the income and expenses of the state land program.

private industry on a sustained yield basis from existing state forest lands. They have sought to assure proper forest fire protection on both state and privately-owned lands, and to provide industrial promotion and service to existing and prospective forest industries. So far timber sales have been very small, now amounting to only around 38 million board feet annually. Sales are increasing slowly each year, providing a few new jobs in the woods and much needed cash income to a number of small and widely scattered part-time operators. But this in no way measures the importance of the present program. Recent economic studies of the nation's growing natural resource requirements between now and the year A.D. 2000 indicate that domestic timber supplies will be wholly inadequate to meet projected demands and that timber supply will constitute a problem greater than any other major category of natural resource materials.[5] This has special implications for Alaska, with its millions of acres of untouched interior forest lands. Moreover, the Japanese market for Alaska forest products appears to be growing, and various Japanese firms are presently studying the feasibility of establishing wood processing plants in Alaska based on the use of timber from state lands. At the present rate of state land selection it is possible that by 1984 the state will own from 30 to 40 million acres of interior forest lands, and by that time the economic climate should have improved sufficiently to warrant large-scale development of forest industries. The relatively small funds being invested in the state forest program today have every prospect of returning high rewards in the form of economic development and increased revenues to the state treasury in the foreseeable future.

Another of the Division's responsibilities has been the development of a state parks and recreation program. Alaska is in an enviable position for it has an opportunity to select and classify as many public recreational areas as may be necessary to avoid the

5. See Hans H. Landsberg, Leonard L. Fischman and Joseph L. Fisher, *Resources in America's Future: Patterns of Requirements and Availabilities, 1960–2000*. Baltimore: Johns Hopkins Press, 1963.

expensive land acquisition programs now plaguing so many of the other states. Prime recreation areas are being selected and classified with an eye to the future, but unfortunately state funds for the planning and development of a parks program have been extremely limited and it has been necessary for the Division to concentrate its efforts in a few meager areas; less than 5,000 acres of state lands had actually been classified for public recreational use by the end of 1965.

There are seven different classes of public recreation land under the Division's program: wilderness areas, scenic parks, recreation areas, historic sites, beaches, parkways, and highway waysides. The highway wayside program, involving the construction of campgrounds and picnic areas, is considered by the state to be of immediate importance in encouraging the growth of the tourist industry, and practically all of the limited funds available for the park program are being invested in this activity. At the time of statehood, the Bureau of Land Management transferred forty-two campgrounds to the state, and these formed the nucleus of the state highway wayside system. During the ensuing years the Division has nearly doubled the number of campgrounds and increased individual camping units fivefold, but the system still can adequately accommodate only about 60 percent of the current visitors. More campgrounds along the major highway network are planned as funds permit, and the Division is cooperating with the state Department of Highways to develop a supplementary series of scenic overlooks and wayside rest stops for which federal matching funds are available. A start has been made in developing a parks and recreation program but much remains to be done if the state is to meet its responsibilities here.

The Division of Lands recently began experimenting with several novel approaches in the sale of certain classes of land for recreation purposes. In the past, sales of private recreation lands have been limited to small lots—usually less than an acre in size—accessible by road from nearby population centers. In 1964 the Division made available for the first time a series of so-called "wilderness estates" on lakes and river-fronts in remote recreation areas accessible only by small boats or by airplanes equipped to land on water. Individual tracts are large—ranging up to forty acres in size—with liberal water frontages, and inaccessibility rather than accessibility is considered their primary ingredient. By these means, the Division is attempting to dramatize Alaska as "an opportunity for the landless, smog-soaked city dweller to enjoy clean air . . . and the joys of the wilderness."[6] In all cases the state will retain widely spaced public recreation sites around the lakes and along the streams to assure public access. While it is too early to evaluate this new program, the extent of interest shown at the first two auctions has been highly encouraging, and the Division plans additional sales in the future. Nearly a hundred tracts were sold during 1965, and although advertising has been limited, out-of-state residents have accounted for about 15 percent of these sales. Some experimental sales are also being undertaken to determine the potential demand for "country estates"—large residential tracts ranging up to twenty acres and accessible by road to population centers, designed for those Alaskans who seek to enjoy the out-of-doors in their everyday living. In another instance, cross-country ski trails and other recreation trails were given permanent right-of-way status in a newly laid out subdivision near Fairbanks. These easements not only preserved important recreation and esthetic values but resulted in greatly increased revenues to the state when the individual lots were sold. This approach, suggested by the people of the region at a hearing held by the Division prior to classification of the tract, illustrates the value of the hearing procedures in keeping the land program responsive to the public. The flexibility built into the state land laws and regulations permits the Division to conduct such trials and experiments to discover how best to use the land in meeting the needs and desires of the people who choose Alaska as their permanent home.

With exploding populations and the encroachment of cities and

6. Alaska Department of Natural Resources, Division of Lands, *Annual Report, 1964*, pp. 20–21.

suburban developments on the rural landscape, many states are finding that their outdoor-hungry people are being prevented by private lands and "keep out" signs from enjoying the streams, lakes, and other bodies of water that are theirs by constitutional right. A farsighted program, launched by the state Department of Fish and Game and carried out in close cooperation with the Division of Lands, is designed to acquire water access sites for public use before such an impossible situation can develop in Alaska. Much information has already been gathered on thousands of potential sites, and several hundred have already been selected and classified for permanent retention by the state. The average site is less than five acres in size although a few are much larger. The program seeks also to acquire and protect as public rights-of-way trails leading off the roads to the water access sites. Highest priority during the first few years has been given to waters around the main cities and towns where growth is occurring rapidly and the problems of maintaining access are the most pressing, but the Department estimates that several hundred thousand lakes and streams throughout Alaska will be evaluated and processed during the next twenty years. Altogether there are over 3 million lakes and other bodies of water in Alaska that support sport fisheries or have other recreational values, a fact that reveals clearly the size and importance of the job to be accomplished. A noteworthy adjunct to the program occurred in 1964 when the Division of Lands issued a public order declaring that all disposals of land bordering lakes or streams "capable of supporting a sport fishery" shall include a pedestrian easement ten feet wide along the shore or rivers' edge to guarantee public ingress and egress at all times. These measures will insure greater freedom for public enjoyment of the waters of Alaska for sport fishing and other outdoor recreational pursuits than exists anywhere else in the United States.

Still other Division activities are aimed at saving money or enhancing state property values rather than at producing immediate revenues. Land has been located and furnished free of charge to various state agencies for building sites and other public needs.

Free use permits for the removal of gravel and other materials have been issued to the Department of Highways and other government agencies, and this alone has resulted in a saving to the state of several million dollars during the last few years. Rights-of-way across state lands are also provided to individuals at a nominal fee or without charge to assist development of state lands; and several hundred free-use permits to allow removal of gravel, timber, and other materials for personal use have been issued when it has been in the interest of the state to do so.

A pioneer access road program, authorized in 1962 by the legislature (122 SLA 1961), permits the Division to contract with private firms for construction of low standard roads that will provide access to state lands and thus enhance their market value. Payment for construction is made with "land credit certificates," valid for twenty years. During this period the certificates can be used either as cash by the road contractor to purchase or lease state lands and resources or they may be sold to other companies or individuals who in turn can use them in any state land transactions. The program allows the state to use the land rather than scarce cash to build access roads, and the Division expects each pioneer road to increase the value of state lands considerably in excess of the value of the certificates. By the end of 1965 over twenty such contracts had been let under the program. As a further inducement, the Division has been empowered to sell or lease state land at a reduced price in exchange for the building of roads that will increase state land values by extending access into underdeveloped areas. These various encouragements have brought over a hundred miles of low standard roads into existence, including timber roads, mineral roads, grazing roads, roads to open up residential and recreational subdivisions, and roads needed for earthquake relocation projects. Many thousands of previously inaccessible acres are now in production or available for use as a result of these efforts.

Before statehood, improvements—particularly salmon canneries—were placed on tidelands when they were held in trust by the federal government and there was no way at all to obtain legal title. These improvements were actually unlawful and in trespass, but as mentioned earlier, state law stipulated that both individuals and municipalities that had developed and improved tidelands before statehood were eligible to receive title. All other tidelands could only be leased; they could not be sold or granted by the state. One of the primary tasks of the Division has been the processing and adjudication of hundreds of these preference right claims, and the furnishing of a clear and assignable title to eligible tideland occupants. Since the law provided that all preference rights expired in 1964, this aspect of the tideland program has received the greatest attention during these first few years. The Division has however sought to encourage the use and development of the tidelands through negotiated and competitive leases, material sales, short-term tideland permits, and rights-of-way and easements required for tideland use. Some 250 miles of shoreline have been classified for their highest and best use, and approximately three-quarters of this total has been designated for public recreation use.

Knowledge of the physical characteristics of Alaska's tidelands is meager, and one of the main objectives of the Division has been to assemble data that will materially aid in the management and development of these lands. Coastal and beach erosion are causing serious losses of land and property in some areas of Alaska, and without funds to conduct detailed studies or construct protective measures, the Division has attempted to attract interest to the problem by circulating technical papers and reports to other organizations and government agencies. Recently the Corps of Engineers launched the first major beach study ever to be conducted along Alaska's great coastline, in the Homer area on the Kenai Peninsula, and it may be hoped that other similar studies can be undertaken in the future, for these lands will undoubtedly prove to be one of the state's most valuable assets.

These are the highlights of the state's land program. More specific details concerning the activities of the Division may be found in the appendix tables. The essential purpose here has been to reveal the broad pattern of program development. The fears expressed before statehood by various groups and individuals—both private and governmental—that the prospective state might immediately squander a large land grant have been in good part quelled by the legislative and administrative policies laid down to guide the Division of Lands during these first years. This does not mean the state land program is flawless or that the future is altogether bright. Sound laws and regulations will not in themselves assure success any more than the quality of a sculptor's tools will guarantee the excellence of his creations. It will be several years before there is sufficient data to make a critical appraisal of the program, but there are, however, a number of current and emerging problems and policy issues which in all probability will have a strong bearing upon the long-term success. A few of the more important and obvious conflicts—many of which have already been alluded to—are presented in the next four chapters. The intent is not to provide a detailed or complete coverage but merely to illustrate the breadth and character of the problems facing the state as it moves ahead with its land program.

Chapter 5

Development vs. Conservation

OVERSHADOWING all other influences on state land policy is the financial crisis confronting the new state government. The political transition from territorialism to statehood has been accompanied by an economic transition which compounds the problems of financing the growing costs of state government, and a brief review of the trends in the Alaska economy will help to understand its relationship to land policy.[1]

Before World War II, Alaska's economy was dependent upon the harvesting, processing, and export of natural resources with three products, furs, canned salmon, and gold forming a narrow and highly specialized base. During this so-called colonial era, population growth was slow and erratic, depending primarily on the ups and downs in the output of these three products. Following 1940, this extractive economy was eclipsed by the rise of the federal military economy as Alaska's strategic military location was recognized and exploited. Over the next two decades billions of dollars were expended in the construction of military bases, improved surface and air transportation, and other public works related to the needs of a huge military establish-

1. For a more detailed analysis of the Alaska economy see George W. Rogers and Richard A. Cooley, *Alaska's Population and Economy: Regional Growth, Development and Future Outlook* (Vol. I—Analysis and Vol. II—Statistical Handbook), University of Alaska Economic Series, Institute of Business, Economic and Government Research, 1963.

ment. This massive federal investment was primarily responsible for the territory's phenomenal population growth and for its increased economic well-being during the forties and fifties. It also contributed greatly to the ultimate political development of statehood.

By 1960, however, changing military technology and defense concepts began to alter the role of the military in Alaska. New emphasis was placed on the specialist, causing a shift away from the ordinary soldier. Armed forces personnel moved out in large

TABLE 3

Alaska's Population Growth, 1880–1965

Year	Total Alaska	Civilian		Military
		(Native)	(Non-native)	
1880	33,426	32,996	430	—
1890	32,052	25,354	6,698	—
1900	63,592	29,542	34,050	—
1910	64,356	25,331	39,025	—
1920	55,036	26,558	28,228	250 *
1930	59,278	29,983	29,045	250 *
1940	72,524	32,458	39,566	500 *
1950	128,643	33,863	74,373	20,407
1960	226,167	43,081	150,394	32,692
1965 *	253,000	49,500	171,500	32,000

* Estimated
Source: U.S. Bureau of the Census

numbers, and military construction declined. This turn of events has resulted in acute unemployment and local economic distress, even though federal expenditures still remain the most important single element in the Alaska economy (federal funds appropriated for Alaska in 1965 amounted to over $500 million). Table 3 shows how these various economic forces have influenced Alaska's growth since 1880. Today the total population of Alaska amounts to about 255,000 people, with over 25 percent representing military personnel and their dependents. Despite the rapid rate of growth during the past two decades, the state is still very sparsely populated, with an average population density of only forty persons to every 100 square miles, compared with the United States average of over 6,000 persons per 100 square miles. In fact, Alaska's sparsity of population in 1965 closely resembles that of the West about a century ago.

For the present and in the immediate future, one of Alaska's most pressing problems is the promotion of a smooth transition from a federal military economy to one again based almost exclusively on its natural resources. But the difficulties are great. The old natural resource props of furs, fish, and gold declined steadily during the forties and fifties as a result of changing demands, costs, and—in the case of salmon—as a result of overfishing which led to severe depletion of the resource. Other natural resources which contributed to the pre-World War II economic base have lessened in value, adding immensely to the difficulties of the economic transition. Between 1911 and 1938 copper ore production was important but since 1938 it has virtually disappeared. A number of other minerals were produced, mostly as by-products of gold and copper, but their total values were never significant over any period of time. Coal, and sand and gravel became important with the advent of the military establishment but are only minor components of the natural resource output.

Fortunately, three major natural resources have emerged since the mid-1950's as dynamic factors in Alaska's economy. Forest products industries, oil and gas exploration and production, and tourism and recreation have expanded greatly. Their continued growth has however been unable to offset completely the decline in other segments of the economy, and Alaska remains in a precarious position with high unemployment rates, a narrow economic base relying heavily on government spending, and an ever-threatening continued downward adjustment in the total superstructure. In a valiant effort to broaden and strengthen the economy, the state government has given much attention to the possibilities of developing other natural resources; but these are still far from fully explored, and reputable local economists and national consulting firms who have studied the available data agree that while the long-term prospects are bright, many of the resources known to exist are either too low in quality or existing production costs are too high to warrant immediate large-scale development.

State government expenditures have increased rapidly during the last few years as Alaska accepted the added responsibilities and costs of statehood. The new land program was launched; the full cost of managing fish and game was assumed; judicial and other purely local and state functions previously performed by the federal government were transferred; and highways, airfields, and other capital needs which formerly had been paid for entirely by the federal government became state responsibilities. To be sure, with these new financial responsibilities there came new sources of revenue, and the Statehood Act provided for federal transitional grants amounting to $30.5 million to help the state through the first few critical years of self-government. Yet the unstable nature of the economy has meant that total revenues from all sources have not increased as rapidly as total expenses, and all the while the budgetary needs of the expanding state government have grown. The crippling earthquake in March, 1964, placed additional unexpected demands upon the state treasury, and these were only partly offset by federal assistance in the form of special earthquake grants to the state.[2] Of necessity the state has placed a strong emphasis on the production of revenues when forming its short-range objectives in the land program. Indeed, a financial crisis would have occurred earlier had not the state received large windfall profits, amounting to over $100 million, from the leasing of state- and federally-owned oil and gas lands. Although these revenues are highly unstable and unpredictable from year to year, they have been used to meet the growing permanent costs of state government. In the last two years this important source of revenue has declined, contributing to the state's financial problems and giving clear warning of the dangers

2. Congress earmarked $23.5 million for this purpose.

of relying on this variable source of income to meet everyday recurring expenses. So far, the state government has been fortunate, but what happens if the oil bonuses fail to materialize?

These comments on the contemporary financial situation have a direct bearing on the state's program for the selection and disposal of its lands. It is true that because Alaska's economy is only beginning to develop, the state has an unprecedented opportunity to draw upon the knowledge and experience of the past in planning for the wise use of its natural resources. But from a practical political standpoint, the immediate need for quick cash to maintain government services may for many years control the formation of land and resource policies. If state revenues remain inadequate the funds available for important resource management and conservation programs may decrease, and pressures may increase for the state to sell or otherwise dispose of its land and natural resources in any way that would bring immediate revenue, with little regard for the long-range consequences. A downward spiral of this nature would have a devastating impact on the state land program. This presents the state of Alaska with a paramount challenge. How can it resolve the conflict between the need for more and faster development of the lands and resources so that the region can become a healthy, productive segment of the United States economy with the need to retain those qualities of wild country, grand scenery, and a hunting and fishing paradise which are its special attributes? [3]

Resolving the conflict will not be easy, for Alaska has attracted an inordinate number of people whose views seem to polarize at either end of a development-conservation spectrum. There are the extreme twentieth-century developers who think of Alaska as a northern extension of the western frontier, and who wish to populate and industrialize it as rapidly as possible. They envy

3. For a discussion of the Division of Lands' viewpoint on this, see Salvatore DeLeonardis and Herbert C. Lang, "Planning for Alaska's Future," article in the 1963 Yearbook of the U.S. Department of Agriculture, *A Place to Live* (Washington: Govt. Printing Office, 1963), p. 509.

California her crowded millions and want to create in Alaska cities like Los Angeles, Chicago, or New York. They see themselves as modern pioneers, and they demand the freedom of action that was given their counterparts a century earlier. To them, any resource use is a good use. But they do not realize that in their zeal they may be sacrificing those unique natural values which in the long run may be the only real values upon which Alaska can build a healthy, productive economy. In short, they may be making mud pies out of gold dust.

At the other end of the spectrum are the extreme conservationists who came to Alaska, for the most part, to get away from the rushing industrial environment the developers wish to create. They believe economic development has gone much too far already, and they are quick to attack any proposal for further development. They prefer an Alaska as wild and unsettled as it was when the United States took it over from Russia. But by following such a negative philosophy they may be defeating their own purpose, for a state in the throes of economic and financial bankruptcy will be in no position to countenance policies of conservation. They may end by killing the goose that lays the golden egg.

Fortunately, an occasional questioning voice points the way toward a blending of these dichotomous views. A recent editorial in the Juneau daily newspaper focused on the real issue. Said the editor:

> The progress (or development) complex has infected Alaska. We are caught firmly in its grip and cannot extricate ourselves. . . . Yet we cannot entirely shrug off the strange whisper that comes sometimes in the night and asks why we must continue to move onward from the peaceful, grassy knoll into an unknown future of dense and swirling population. Who has carefully considered the situation and decided that Alaska would be better with a million people, or two million people, than with the present two hundred and thirty thousand? In what way will it be better? Will it be better for you individually or for your friends and neighbors? Will you enjoy Alaska more then—its beautiful mountains and glaciers, its coastlines and tundra, its recreational opportunities? Will you find it easier to pay your bills? Will the state government? . . .
>
> We cannot and would not halt the march of time, but let us to the extent

possible, move forward with farseeing eyes, striving to guide the bandwagon instead of riding it blindly toward some strange place and condition that may not be as desirable, in truth, as where we are today.[4]

A large majority of the people in Alaska would probably agree with this more cautious approach to the future. But while this less vociferous majority holds the balance of political power, it has not yet entered the arena and joined the battle. It is this group that must stir into action if Alaska is to use its great land patrimony wisely, for it is no play on words to say that development and conservation can and must move ahead together if the state is to carve out a future that encourages rather than destroys those natural and human qualities that now make Alaska unique among the fifty states. As Stewart Udall phrased it, "Conservation statesmen must prove that profits and the conservation cause are compatible if we are to succeed in making an attractive and orderly environment part of our national purpose." [5]

The state confronts a much more difficult problem in land selection than first meets the eye. During the first few years of statehood considerable lands with known economic values were available for selection around the centers of population, and the choice was fairly easy. From Map 6, showing existing state selections, however, it is readily apparent that nearly all of these lands have now been taken. As the state moves further into the hinterlands in its selections, the quality and completeness of technical information about the land and its resources diminish and it is becoming more difficult to render sound decisions. In fact, there is some conjecture today as to whether the state will be able to locate lands of sufficient value in the public domain during the next two decades to permit it to take full advantage of the liberal land grant provisions.

Many areas of potentially high value are not available for selection at present since they are reserved by the federal government. As mentioned earlier, federal reserves encompass

4. Darwin Lambert, in the *Daily Alaska Empire,* July 8, 1962.

5. Stewart Udall, *The Quiet Crisis* (New York: Holt, Rinehart and Winston, 1963), p. 183.

over 100 million acres and none of this land is open to state selection, except for 400,000 acres from the national forests for community expansion and recreation. In addition, there are large land areas that undoubtedly will never be considered suitable for large-scale selection because of adverse physical features. This includes areas of high mountains and glaciers—generally above the 3,000 foot elevation contour—and extensive areas of swamp land, muskeg and tundra. Some mountain areas may be desirable for state parks and recreation sites, but it is unlikely that this would involve extensive acreages. Others might become valuable because of the presence of minerals, but again it is not likely that the state would choose to select on a large scale for this single purpose, since it is already guaranteed 90 percent of all revenues from the production of minerals on federal lands. (Of course in this era of expanding populations and rapid technological change, today's wastelands eventually might become tomorrow's promised lands, but this discussion must be concerned only with the foreseeable future.) Taking into account these physical and economic factors, probably less than 40 million acres of land are presently worthy of any consideration for state selection, and the lack of solid resource surveys over much of Alaska makes it extremely difficult to predict which of these will have the greatest potential value for multiple use. As a matter of fact, some authorities believe it unlikely that the state will be able to find more than 25 million acres worthy of selection before the cut-off date in 1984. If these predictions prove true, Alaska will perhaps want to ask Congress to extend the period another ten or fifteen years.

To many a casual observer it seems impossible that the state could lose on land given to it free. What they overlook is that land ownership results in direct costs to the state, not only in selecting the land, but in the funds which must be provided annually for fire protection and other minimum management obligations. For lands slated to be sold or leased, there are further costs of surveying, classifying, appraising, and conducting auctions. And there are other, indirect costs. Federal highway matching funds are computed on the basis of the percentage of federal lands within the state, and when land is removed from the federal public domain through state selection, the effect is to reduce the federal contributions for highway construction. This alone results in a loss of income to the state of about eight cents for every acre selected. The present state selection of 17 million acres, for example, results in an annual loss of about $1½ million in highway matching funds, and this will increase by about $300,000 a year at the present rate of state land selection.

Taking into account all of these factors, it costs the state at the very least an estimated ten to twelve cents a year for each acre of land selected. This mounts to no small expense considering the millions of acres involved. If the state selected land at the rate of 5 million acres a year—the approximate average rate required if it takes all of the land grant within the allotted time—its costs would increase by an additional half-million dollars each year. Over a ten-year period the total cumulative expense of gaining 40 million acres of land would be approximately $27½ million, if one assumes that no land is sold or leased. In this hypothetical example, the actual out-of-pocket expenses are approximately $9 million while the remaining $18 million amounts to the loss in federal highway matching funds. It is not technically correct to combine the two since the latter represents a loss of revenue rather than a direct cost of land selection and management, but since the state will undoubtedly continue to match all of these federal funds because of the lucrative 19 to 1 matching formula, it may be considered a direct cost for all practical purposes. Furthermore, after the ten-year period the state would be faced with recurrent annual management costs of about $2 million a year as long as these lands remained in state ownership.

It is imperative that the state exercises great discretion and judgment, and that it does not blindly select land for the mere sake of massive ownership. As one spokesman for the Division of Lands put it, "Without proper planning the generosity of the granter could prove to be the undoing of the receiver. . . . Tomorrow the state could enjoy a continual and uninterrupted flow of income generated by a good land ownership pattern, or it could be saddled with unburdenable expenses."[6] The state's only rational alternative is to move ahead slowly and cautiously, always balancing anticipated land values against the costs of assuming the financial obligations of land management. The more it can prolong the process of selection, the more information there will be upon which choices can be made, and the smaller will be the financial burden of land ownership to the state.

6. Herbert C. Lang, "Progress in State Administration: Selection Policy Considerations." *Science in Alaska 1962.* Proceedings of the Fourteenth Alaskan Science Conference, Anchorage, Alaska, August 27–30, 1963 (Alaska Division A. A. A. S., 1964), p. 4.

Chapter 6

Patterns of Settlement

FROM the emotionally charged question of native land rights have emerged problems of tremendous complexity, problems that not only bear strongly on evolving patterns of land ownership and land-use in Alaska but could eventually undermine the entire state land program unless equitable solutions are found.

The 1867 treaty in which Alaska was acquired by the United States failed to define the entitlement of the Indians, Aleuts, and Eskimos to lands they were using and occupying, and since that date Congress has sidestepped the issue. Few Indian reservations of the type so freely created throughout the United States in the nineteenth century have been established in Alaska, but since 1900, large acreages have been withdrawn from the public domain for native use and occupancy, and for the establishment of schools, hospitals, and other programs of benefit to the natives. The extent of the natives' rights to much of this land is uncertain. Two minor pieces of federal legislation gave individual natives in Alaska special opportunities to acquire title to small tracts for which they could prove use and occupancy over a period of years: the Alaska Native Allotment Act of 1906 (34 U.S. Stat., 197) allows each native to obtain a restricted title to as much as 160 acres of nontaxable and inalienable land for the personal use of himself and his heirs in perpetuity, and the Alaska Native Townsite Act of 1926 (44 U.S. Stat., 629) made it possible for natives to obtain similar restrictive titles to lots they were occupying in surveyed townsites. But the basic issue of native land rights is far from settled.

Today, as a consequence of congressional indecision on the question of aboriginal land rights, the state is finding an increasing number of its land selections challenged and protested by native groups. There is no mechanism for the adjudication of these cases, and a single native protest results in the Department of the Interior in 1965, indefinitely suspending all action leading to transfer of land to the state. Of the nearly 5 million acres of state land selections waiting tentative approval from the Department of the Interior in 1965, over 75 percent was tied up in this way, and the problem gets worse from year to year as the state moves further into the hinterland with its selections. "Eskimos Claim Half of Alaska," read a banner newspaper headline in January, 1966, and the article dramatically illustrates the magnitude of the dilemma.[1] An organization known as the North Slope Native Association has officially protested the state of Alaska's selection of land in the arctic and is claiming all revenues from the land for the Eskimo residents of the region. The land in question recently came under intensive exploration by major oil companies. Geologists believe the odds for large commercial discoveries are excellent, and this had led the state to begin land selections in anticipation of large revenues from the leasing activities. The attorney for the Eskimo group stated:

> I filed protest with the state on the grounds that the land belongs to the Eskimos on the basis of aboriginal title. All oil land is granted through the public land law. I hold the law is clear on this point—that it is not public land unless the aboriginal title has been extinguished. . . . We don't want to stop the exploration of Alaska but just have the money for exploration rights paid to the natives and not the government.

This one protest alone encompasses more than 96 million acres. Map 7 shows other areas throughout Alaska subject to similar native claims. A comparison of this map with others showing

1. *Seattle Post Intelligencer,* January 25, 1966.

lands with known resource values that are currently open for state selection exposes the full gravity of the situation.

The complexity of the native land problem stems from the special land-use requirements of these people. Many of the Indian, Aleuts, and Eskimos still rely heavily upon wildlife resources for food, clothing, and other material necessities. In arctic Alaska Eskimo and wildlife are still closely linked in a natural ecological arrangement which has been disturbed very little until recent years. Here small and frequently irregular cash incomes supplement subsistence village economies which are very nearly self-sufficient, based upon the harvesting of mammals, berries, fish, birds, eggs, and other available resources. Under present economic and social conditions these people cannot survive without wildlife. A recent federal Task Force on Alaska native affairs summarized the problem in the following manner:

> Those who espouse the cause of the natives express concern that lands near the native villages may pass into the hands of the state . . . and that as a result of increasing mineral explorations, dam construction, the promotion of tourism, etc., the natives will lose access to areas upon which they now depend for their subsistence hunting and fishing.[2]

The Task Force noted that the Alaska Native Allotment Act, which resembled the federal Homestead Act in many ways, was scarcely suitable for hunters who live in villages often far removed from the land upon which they seek their quarry. They concluded:

> The State of Alaska is genuinely concerned that aboriginal claims brought by Indians, Eskimos and Aleuts may delay transfer of title in the case of lands which they select pursuant to the Statehood Act. Some of those with whom members of the Task Force discussed the problem indicated they would prefer that determination of these claims be deferred for the present, and at a later date heard before a special tribunal (similar to the Indian Claims Commission) which Congress might establish for that purpose. Thus, the State would be able to acquire income-producing lands, which it badly needs, and the Indians would presumably be compensated

2. "Report to the Secretary of the Interior by the Task Force on Alaska Native Affairs," Dec. 28, 1962 (mimeo), p. 62.

for the loss of whichever of these lands they could establish valid claim to under the doctrine of aboriginal rights.

There are several objections which the Indian defense groups pose to that position. To begin with, they contend that the economy of many native groups would be seriously disrupted if the lands already selected or certain to be selected, by the State were to be transferred from the public domain without any ironclad assurance that Indian hunting and fishing rights in these areas would be protected. Thus, the natives would be trading their present way of life for a vague promise of future money payments which, while compensating them for the worth of the land, might not compensate them for the destruction of their economy. The land is primarily useful to them at present only for hunting and fishing, activities whose financial value would be difficult to compute.[3]

In its final recommendations, the Task Force emphasized that the reservation of large acreages of land for the exclusive use of the natives was not in the best interests of either the state or the natives. They suggested instead that the state and federal governments consider designating "subsistence use areas" where natives and other persons who depend upon hunting, fishing, and berry picking for their subsistence would have a continuing privileged claim to the harvest of these natural products. This could be accomplished through establishment of a special land classification category by the state; or it could be accomplished by reserving the right to hunt, fish, and harvest wild foods to the state, as is now done with mineral rights. Under this latter alternative, title to the land could pass to private ownership but the right to gather resources for subsistence would remain open to all.

The Task Force recommended that the Alaska Native Allotment Act should be more liberally administered by the Bureau of Land Management. The act, they agreed, would more nearly meet native needs if each native, instead of being limited to a single 160-acre tract as he has been in the past, was allowed to receive title to his camp site, his fishing and hunting site, and his homesite, as long as the total individual allotment did not exceed the maximum 160 acres provided in the legislation. The Task Force also suggested that the state forego selection of lands in the

3. *Ibid.*, pp. 66–67.

immediate vicinity of native villages for the time being in order to give the inhabitants an opportunity to obtain small acreages for their permanent use and occupancy under the provisions of this federal act. Both the state and federal governments have subsequently adopted these recommendations to a large extent, though complications are still arising.

The Task Force also called attention to the confusion surrounding rights to lands already reserved for native use. Many native communities have been unable to make use of the resources these reserves contain because of the uncertain legal status of the land, and this it considered unfortunate for both the natives and the state government. To overcome this problem, it was recommended that the Interior Department seek authority from Congress to lease or otherwise develop these lands for the benefit of the natives. Finally the Task Force recommended that Congress take immediate steps to clarify aboriginal land rights in Alaska, and, if necessary, to establish a tribunal to hear and adjudicate native claims. Unless Congress acts soon on these recommendations the state land program will be placed in serious jeopardy, for it is obvious from the foregoing that much of the land contemplated for selection is subject to these aboriginal claims; and an equitable resolution would greatly aid the natives in the difficult cultural and economic transition in which they are presently engrossed.

Even when aboriginal land rights are clarified, the state will still be confronted with the need for a complete reevaluation of land policy as it relates to agricultural settlement in Alaska. The state's great land area has given rise to perennial dreams of large-scale agricultural development. After all, so the argument generally goes, land for agriculture was the primary force stimulating settlement and population growth in the West. Why not in Alaska? Some even make the assertion that every underdeveloped region must pass through an agricultural stage before it can graduate to a higher order of industrial development and economic growth; and that land policy in Alaska should encourage—indeed, if necessary, subsidize—agricultural settlement at this early stage of the region's development. This contention is bolstered by that deep-rooted belief, lying behind the Homestead Act of the last century, that every man should have a right to try his luck at establishing a small farm on public lands because there is something inherently good in such pioneering efforts. These beliefs were responsible for the unique provision placed in the federal Homestead Act for Alaska allowing the settler to select land anywhere on the open public domain regardless of whether the land had been surveyed or classified as suitable for agricultural use; they were also instrumental in the state's decision to adopt its own homestead law, with its credit system and its other special inducements for the man with little capital who wants to try his hand at pioneering.

It is generally agreed that homesteading served an important purpose in the West of the nineteenth century. But the physical and economic conditions of Alaska in the twentieth century are in no way comparable. The economics of pioneering used to be simple. Capital requirements were small, low standards of living were accepted, and the homesteader was willing to work from dawn to dark, to live in isolation and to do without schools, police protection, and doctors. There was a wide gap between production costs and market price, and the chief problem was one of getting the product to market. In Alaska today, however, the local farmer-settler is confronted with very high capital and labor costs, small local markets for the few agricultural products his land will produce, and stiff competition from low-priced products shipped in from highly mechanized farming regions of the West and Midwest. Current estimates for the capital requirements to establish a minimum-sized farm in Alaska range from $40,000 to $65,000. It is reprehensible for government policy to mislead the homesteader into believing he can set up a commercial enterprise on the basis of a meager savings account—or from the surplus income from other employment—when the chances of failure are so very high. An investigation of federal homesteads in one important agricultural region of Alaska showed that about 60 percent had been abandoned or were unoccupied, and another

30 percent were being used solely for residential purposes.[4] The situation is no different with respect to homesteading of state lands.

The social costs of this pattern of land settlement can be very high. Unlike his nineteenth century counterpart, the modern pioneer demands relatively large governmental expenditures for roads, post offices, schools, electricity, police protection, and other public facilities that are today considered necessities; yet he contributes little revenue in the form of taxes. State laws and regulations overcome many of the deficiencies of the federal homestead program, but still it is by no means clear that public and private benefits exceed the costs.

There is sufficient evidence to demonstrate that a large array of crops and livestock can be produced on Alaska's existing physical base of soils, drainage, climate, and terrain. Estimates of total land suitable for crops or cultivated pastures range up to three million acres; only a small fraction of this is now being utilized, and Alaska is presently producing less than 10 percent of its total consumption of agricultural products. In spite of these favorable factors, it is highly unlikely that agriculture will ever become a major industry in Alaska; instead, development will occur very slowly as local markets expand and economic conditions warrant. In the meantime, there is need for complete reevaluation of land settlement policies to prevent unnecessary waste of natural, human, and economic resources in agricultural endeavors that are destined to fail from the beginning. In contemplating the broad land-use pattern emerging in Alaska, and the various factors and forces influencing it, a suggestion by one economist is especially intriguing:

> Just as public policy in the last century found a more or less tangible object (cheap land) to meet its . . . vague and imperfectly understood basic needs, public policy in this century has begun to recognize what we broadly define as "recreation resources" to be the tangible object which

4. Hugh A. Johnson and Robert Coffman, *Land Occupancy, Ownership and Use on Homesteads in the Kenai Peninsula, Alaska 1955* (Alaska Agricultural Experiment Station, Bul. 21, Nov. 1956), p. 8.

appears to meet contemporary needs. . . . What tracts of free or cheap agricultural lands meant in the development of our far western territories during the last century, recreation resources could mean in Alaska's future development. In each example, the key resource group is something which satisfied a very intense current hunger of men of each age. Just as agricultural resources provided a broad economic base for the regions having them in past ages, so recreation resources by their very variety and the broadness of the needs they meet would be reflected in a corresponding broadening of Alaska's economic base in the present age. Properly recognized, conserved and developed as the need emerges, Alaska can here find the added element which could give it the type of balanced development long hoped for.[5]

With statehood, Alaska became eligible for financial assistance under the Federal Highway Act (Public Law 84–627), and because the matching ratio is based on the proportion of federal lands within each state, Alaska is in a very favorable position: for every dollar the state puts up for highway construction, the federal government donates approximately $19 in matching funds. This has created a strong inducement for the state to take all of the federal funds available to it each year under the terms of the act, and since statehood the highway construction program has been by far the largest item in the state's total budget, amounting to an average of around $40 million annually. In addition, the state must pay the full costs of maintaining the highway system, which is no small item in itself. The question can be raised as to whether this lucrative federal matching ratio has led to an imbalance in state budgeting, but that is not the principal issue to be discussed here. The state does need roads and undoubtedly it will continue to take advantage of the provisions in the Federal Highway Act as long as the matching ratio remains so profitable.

Of greater importance in relation to land policy is that the highway construction program is being carried forward at a rapid pace with little regard to the impact on land and resource development. Current highway planning is limited almost entirely to an engineering analysis—on a project-by-project basis—

5. George W. Rogers, "Alaska's Recreation Potential," unpublished manuscript prepared for the National Park Service, 1956, p. 8.

Source: Bureau of Land Management

Yentna Glacier, cutting south through the rugged Alaska Range

Source: State of Alaska

Despite its barren appearance, the arctic provides subsistence for Eskimo and wildlife alike

Dense forests of spruce and hemlock in the Tongass National Forest

Source: State of Alaska

Geese and other migratory birds on the Chickaloon Flats

Source: U.S. Fish and Wildlife Service

Source: Bureau of Land Manag

Bears are the least able of all big game to withstand the spread of settle

Whiteface Herefords on Kodiak Island

Source: State of

New techniques greatly reduce the time and cost of survey in Alaska

Source: Bureau of Land Management

New highway near Anchorage

Source: State of Alaska

Shantytowns have sprung up on the edges of Alaska's cities

Source: State of Alaska

Source: Alaska Division of Lands

Oil Refinery on the Kenai Peninsula

Abandoned military base in the Aleutian Islands

Source: State of Alaska

Source: U.S. Fish and Wildlife Service

The alpine tundra provides a unique wilderness experience

A canoe trail in the Kenai National Moose Range

Source: U.S. Fish and Wildlife Service

of how to build a highway from point A to point B as rapidly and efficiently as possible. Transportation is one of the most powerful tools available for shaping the use of land, yet in planning the highway system in Alaska the Department of Highways has made almost no effort to coordinate its program with the Department of Economic Development and Planning, the Department of Fish and Game, and the Department of Natural Resources. These three agencies and several federal offices cannot properly perform their functions to protect and develop the lands and resources under their jurisdiction if highway planning is allowed to remain an autonomous operation within a single agency where decisions are so heavily based on engineering criteria. The public is faced with a question of basic policy. How can it forge a highway system that will provide the greatest possible aid to resource development, and foster desirable land-use patterns rather than distort them?

After an intensive study of the transportation requirements of developing countries around the world, Wilfred Owen of the Brookings Institute drew the following conclusion:

> Transportation policies that make sense have to be derived from development objectives that also make sense. The most urgent need is to create a new state of mind in which transport decisions are clearly seen as an integral part of other policy decisions. To do this will mean giving up some global misconceptions about the transport function.
>
> The mistake that causes the most trouble is the view that transport is a separate sector of the economy. In reality, it is not a sector but a link among sectors. As a consequence, the idea that transport should be improved for its own sake is erroneous. Actually, the only justification for providing transport lies in serving other objectives. Transport cannot be planned and managed in isolation, for what is done or not done to provide mobility and access will often determine the success or failure of the development effort.[6]

Surface transportation in Alaska consists of a skeletal system of highways less than 3,500 miles in extent, but expansion is occurring rapidly. Land and resource values can be greatly enhanced or they can be seriously harmed by the shape the

6. Wilfred Owen, *Strategy for Mobility: Transportation for the Developing Countries* (New York: The Brookings Institute, 1964), p. 192.

highway network will take during the coming decades. The state's unique physical and economic conditions demand new approaches, rather than a reliance on methods and techniques in highway planning geared to the requirements of urban America. Legislation should be considered, for example, to allow use of federal highway matching funds in Alaska without the normally required high standards of construction. This would allow the state to build more miles of lower standard roads designed to make potential resources accessible for exploration and development. Congress might also consider diverting a larger share of the matching funds into basic research and planning, including perhaps resource inventories where the information is of critical importance in highway location, or into construction of other forms of transportation more appropriate to Alaska's needs. The situation calls desperately for a kind of coordinated planning—a strategy for mobility—that does not now exist.

Chapter 7

Conflicts in Resource Use

AS the amount of state-owned land increases, conflicts over the use of the land arise. What, for instance, is of the greatest value to Alaska—cattle or brown bear? On Kodiak Island there lives the largest community of an increasingly rare specimen, the so-called Kodiak brown bear. This, the biggest bear on earth, is both a coveted trophy and a source of interest and wonder to many whose ambition is to observe rather than to kill. But the Kodiak area also contains some of the state's best grazing lands, and during the last decade a livestock industry has begun to develop. Transportation, one of the keys to the success of this industry, is being improved rapidly, so that economic pressures for larger grazing areas are developing. At the same time, the guides, sportsmen, and conservationists, realizing that the brown bear are the least able of all big game species to meet the onslaught of civilization, are anxious to protect the bear population on the Island. The state recently selected lands in this area and applications for grazing leases have been filed by private groups. The lands have not yet been classified for their highest and best use, but it will be necessary to come to a decision very soon. The immediate direct cash values of the grazing leases to the state would be minimal, but to local governmental units cows are more readily taxable than brown bear.

Much of the public controversy that has flared over this issue has been generated by prejudice or incomplete information. And there are similar potential conflicts where research is needed before the matter becomes more serious: commercial reindeer herds conflict with caribou grazing and waterfowl nesting; salmon with logging; and moose with oil exploration and production. Some limited research is currently being conducted in all three of these fields. In 1949 the Forest Service began to examine the effects of logging on salmon, and coordinated measures to avoid damage to moose range in oil exploration and development on the Kenai National Moose Range have been well handled so far. Nevertheless, continuing research on a larger scale is needed to avoid or reduce possible conflicts in the multiple use of lands and resources as the state develops. Because there are as yet no definite answers, for example, to the question of the impact of logging on fish, the Alaska Department of Fish and Game has been forced to take a defensive approach and assume the worst, in view of the unfortunate history of the fisheries in other Pacific Coast states. A comprehensive study of the place of wildlife in the Alaska economy could do much to place these issues in their proper perspective. It would be a great loss to Alaska and the nation if the economic and esthetic values of these resources are not given full consideration in the development of the state, for in the long run wild fish and game, and the opportunity for wilderness recreation, may offer the highest use to which much of the land can be put. Research in this area can help to mitigate conflict and provide the basis for meaningful decisions on the best possible uses of lands and resources.

To insure that wild game will be available for public observation in the various regions of Alaska, the Department of Fish and Game has established a series of "closed areas" in which the taking of certain fish or game species is prohibited. Most of these have fragile habitats which can easily be destroyed by certain types of development, but the Department has no control whatever over the land uses that may occur there, and without some regulation there is no assurance that these areas can be preserved. If the state wishes to give greater protection to important wildlife habitats, it has only two alternatives under present state law:

classify the area for public recreation use and establish a state park, or attempt to obtain approval from the legislature for the establishment of a game sanctuary. In many cases, neither is altogether suitable or feasible, particularly as the State Land Act, in reaction against single-purpose reservations of land in the federal period, provides that no land area larger than 640 acres can be withdrawn from the state public domain and reserved for a single-purpose use except by approval of the legislature.[1]

To meet the needs of wildlife protection without unduly limiting other compatible resource uses, the state would be well advised to consider establishing a land classification similar to the "prime habitat zone" presently in use by the Forest Service in its multiple use management plans for the two national forests in Alaska. These zones are defined as areas of exceptional habitats where wildlife is recognized as the key resource.[2] They include important waterfowl resting, feeding, and nesting areas; wildlife refuges; cooperative wildlife management areas; all or part of the watersheds of highly rated salmon spawning streams; and other areas where one or more species are to be given special consideration. The Forest Service permits other uses to the extent that wildlife values receive primary consideration. Public and private recreation developments ordinarily will not be allowed except for simple wildlife-use facilities, but both grazing of domestic livestock and timber cutting is permitted where conflicts with the wildlife resource will not occur. Logging camps and log dumps must be planned to avoid conflicts, and water impoundment plans are coordinated to provide for wildlife needs. Mineral entry is allowed but special precautions are taken to prevent the en-

1. At the present time only one such game sanctuary has been established. This was the Walrus Islands preserve which was set aside in 1960 by the Legislature (115 SLA 1960) at the request of the Department of Fish and Game. Herds of two or three thousand walrus haul out and spend summers on these islands, the only area left in Alaska where this occurs regularly on a large scale. The walrus have abandoned most other areas because of harassment or destruction of their environment.

2. U.S. Forest Service, "Multiple-Use Management Guide for the Alaska Region," Juneau, Alaska, April, 1964 (processed), Ch. 460.

dangering of wildlife values. Road crossings of these zones are kept to a minimum, and in all cases paramount attention is required in location and construction to avoid watershed and wildlife habitat damage. Such an approach recognizes the unique position of wildlife in Alaska's development. Were the Division of Lands to adopt a similar classification, it would raise this form of land use to the level of importance it merits. And in this case the Department of Fish and Game should play a key role in the selection and classification of such lands as well as in the development of criteria for their multiple use.

Since statehood, the Forest Service, the Department of Fish and Game, and the Department of Natural Resources (Division of Lands) have entered into two cooperative agreements for the joint protection of lands primarily valuable for game management.[3] Both the Stikine River Waterfowl Management Area on the coast of southeast Alaska and the Copper River Delta Game Management Area on the coast of southcentral Alaska are prime waterfowl nesting and feeding areas, the latter supporting one of the largest known concentrations of nesting trumpeter swans in North America, many waterfowl and shore birds, and moose, brown bear, deer, and several species of small game and fur animals. Both areas offer excellent hunting, fishing, trapping, and recreational opportunities. The uplands within the designated areas are in the national forests, and are under the administrative jurisdiction of the Forest Service, while the abutting tidelands are state lands and are under the jurisdiction of the Department of Natural Resources. The Forest Service has classified the uplands as prime habitat zones which are managed to protect the breeding, resting, and feeding grounds of the waterfowl and other wildlife of the two areas; the Division of Lands has classified the tidelands as public recreation lands with wildlife recognized as the primary resource of the areas; and the Department of Fish and Game has agreed to regulate hunting and fishing so that it will be compatible with the maintenance of the habitat. Under

3. Cooperative Agreements dated April 10, 1960, and April 5, 1962.

these two cooperative federal-state management plans, leasing or other use of the land is permitted only under tight supervision and control. This is imaginative joint planning at its best. Similar wildlife management areas should be established as soon as possible to protect other important habitat areas throughout Alaska. As Secretary of the Interior Stewart Udall recently wrote, "In Alaska we have a magnificent opportunity to show more respect for wilderness and wildlife values than did our forebears. The wonders of the wilderness still abound there; if we spoil them, we cannot excuse their defilement with pleas of ignorance."[4]

Alaska is exceptionally rich in water resources, but conflicts over the use of the water and the maintenance of its quality will have an important bearing upon land use as the state develops. The mining and logging interests prefer minimum restrictions on the appropriation and use of water. They are at odds with the Department of Fish and Game, which has proposed a system of water reservations and other regulations designed to prevent damaging disturbances to fish and wildlife resources. Other conflicts have emerged over the state's program to preserve public access to waters of high recreation value; over water drainage and pollution control; over the impact of underwater seismic blasts on marine life; and over the extent of consideration to be given fish and wildlife in hydroelectric projects, the proposed Rampart Dam on the Yukon River providing a current example of this controversy. With proper planning in the early stages of development, Alaska can avoid many of the water problems now plaguing other regions of the United States. To be sure, experiences of the other states can be drawn upon, but the whole arctic and subarctic environment gives rise to unique physical conditions and economic and social values for which new guidelines must be developed. There is immediate need for analyses of the problems of harmonizing and adjudicating competing use, taking into consideration the peculiar conditions in Alaska; and there is need

4. Stewart Udall, *The Quiet Crisis* (New York: Holt, Rinehart and Winston, 1963), p. 182.

for a compromise water code that protects the public interest in the state's water resources without undue restriction on legitimate resource development.

Ten government agencies presently are gathering hydrologic data and making isolated investigations in Alaska, but no one agency is able to take a comprehensive view of the situation, and there has been little coordinated or wide-ranging research. Recently efforts were initiated to coordinate water investigation in Alaska, and a ten-year master plan for the collection of data has been drafted by an Inter-Agency Technical Committee for Alaska composed of the following agencies:

Federal

Department of the Army
Corps of Engineers

Department of the Interior
Geological Survey
Fish and Wildlife Sevice
Bureau of Reclamation

Department of Health, Education, and Welfare
Public Health Service

Department of Agriculture
Forest Service
Soil Conservation Service
Agricultural Experiment Station

Department of Commerce
Weather Bureau
Bureau of Public Roads

State

Department of Health and Welfare

Department of Natural Resources

Department of Fish and Game
University of Alaska

The committee is sponsored by the Federal Inter-Agency Committee on water resources at the national level. It remains to be seen however whether this group will go beyond the mere collection of basic climatological and hydrological data to carry out coordinated planning in these controversial areas. At the present time decisions on water use are based almost entirely upon the result of pressure group activities. A series of well-planned studies carried out jointly by the various government agencies and interest groups is needed if Alaska is to adopt a sound, comprehensive water management plan before irreparable harm has been done.

At present four federal and three state agencies are directly involved in the development and management of Alaska's recreation lands. In a special report on Alaska, the Outdoor Recreation Resources Review Commission recommended that the state government take the initiative to coordinate the activities of these and other agencies having ancillary duties affecting recreation, and that a unified recreation program should be integrated into a general plan for the economic development of Alaska.[5] Unfortunately, state planning on the scale envisioned in the report has not materialized. Recognizing the dire need for some kind of coordination, representatives from a number of federal and state recreation agencies met early in 1964 to form the Alaska Outdoor Recreation Council. The group has little authority except through voluntary cooperation and mutual exchange of information; and funds for both planning and development of new recreational facilities have been meager.

Despite these organizational and financial limitations, some progress has been made. During the last two years the Branch of Forestry and Recreation in the Division of Lands, with the guidance of the Council and assistance from the federal Bureau of Outdoor Recreation, has taken the initiative in drawing up a preliminary recreation plan for Alaska. This preliminary plan will qualify the state to receive federal matching funds under provisions of the Land and Water Conservation Fund Act (78 U.S. Stat., 895), a new program administered by the Bureau of Outdoor Recreation which provides grants to the states on a fifty-fifty matching basis for purposes of planning, acquisition, and development of public recreation lands and facilities. (The fund is largely derived from admission and user charges at federal

5. Wallace D. Bowman, *Alaska's Outdoor Recreation Potential,* A Report to the Outdoor Recreation Resources Review Commission (ORRRC Study Report No. 9), Washington, D.C., p. 4.

recreation areas and revenues from federal taxes on motorboat fuels; but a prerequisite to receiving these grants is the preparation of a comprehensive statewide outdoor recreation plan.) As more of these federal funds become available to the state, it will be necessary to raise recreation planning to a much higher level in the governmental hierarchy, for a truly unified federal-state plan cannot be developed and executed under the present organizational handicaps. Meanwhile, these early efforts represent a step in the right direction and when the policymakers and the people of Alaska awaken to the great importance of outdoor recreation in the nation's future, much more rapid progress will be made.

The Division of Lands urgently needs guidelines to help it determine the location, amount, and type of recreation lands the state should select to meet long-term requirements. A thorough study of present and anticipated future demands for Alaska's outdoor recreation resources, considering both the volume and the kinds of uses expected by residents and out-of-state visitors, is needed to provide the Division with meaningful criteria for selection and classification. Data from the study would also be extremely useful to planners and policymakers in estimating the probable economic impact of alternative levels of investment in the state's recreation program. The Division has already selected substantial areas of land which appear predominantly suited to recreation uses, and though it has not yet classified most of this land, it has attempted to protect it from immediate private appropriation to allow for an adequate planning period. What should be the relation between private or commercial recreation development and the preservation of recreation areas for public use? Some of these lands have mineral, timber, and other potential values. How can the state balance multiple demands and set priorities without spoiling the recreational values? Can compatible and incompatible uses be defined? The Division of Lands is most interested in research programs that will develop guidelines for public policy and standards for decisions, but state funds for this purpose are meager.

A case in point is the Wood River–Tikchik Lakes area, comprising about 1½ million acres of superb, wild, and remote land in southwestern Alaska selected by the state in 1961. The area is inaccessible except by small float plane but in the future its recreation resources can become an integral part of the state park system. Use of this splendid area can be effectively planned only if some of the fundamental relationships among various potential values are thought through in advance. The need for action is immediate, for these lands cannot long be withheld from private appropriation and commercial exploitation unless in conformity with a meaningful plan. A pilot study of this region would be eminently appropriate, and would establish principles applicable to other similar areas that may be chosen in the eighteen years remaining for land selection. Given the national trends, it is certain that the demands for Alaska's vast and varied outdoor recreation resources will increase mightily in the years ahead, and with proper care the state should be able to avoid the necessity now facing many states of spending huge sums of money to purchase private lands to meet their growing recreation needs. Starting out as it is with a relatively clean slate, the state has an ideal opportunity not only to provide its growing population with adequate open spaces and a system of parks and recreation areas second to none, but to ensure that they receive the full economic benefits of a healthy, growing tourist industry.

Forests, wildlife, water resources, recreation lands—these constitute one interrelated set of problems. And all the issues of upland management must be faced and examined anew in a different context, that of Alaska's vast tidelands. Here too there is urgent need for an inventory and appraisal of physical characteristics and resources. Of particular urgency is the need to locate and protect, through classification, two types of tidelands that are of critical importance to the future development of the state. First, the many beaches and other areas of natural beauty, especially near the major coastal cities, should be classified to insure the greatest possible public enjoyment of their value. Second, potential industrial sites along the tidewater are scarce and require some kind of protection to insure that economic development in the various regions of Alaska will not be impeded in the years ahead. Such a thing could easily happen if these prime sites are leased or otherwise disposed of by the state or federal government for purposes of lesser importance. Only certain choice portions of the tidelands can meet the special physical, economic, and locational requirements for these two land uses, and it is imperative that action be taken before the opportunity is lost. This will require close cooperation between the Division of Lands and the various local government units having tidelands within their boundaries, as well as several federal agencies. In nearly all cases, a portion of the uplands must be given a similar classification to protect the primary purpose.

A policy adopted by the Forest Service in the Tongass National Forest of southeastern Alaska should be considered by the state as a possible means of classifying and protecting important scenic values on parts of the tidelands and adjacent lands. In the multiple use management plans for this region, the Forest Service has established "water influence zones"—narrow strips of land along streams, lakes, and seashores where recreational uses will be concentrated, or where people customarily travel the water for pleasure and sport. They are managed to preserve waterfront vegetation, scenic attractions, and esthetic values, and are kept open for unrestricted public access and enjoyment. Other resource uses are allowed only if compatible with maintaining these primary values. The Forest Service has also established special "steamer lane zones" in which timber harvesting and other extensive land uses are strictly controlled so that travelers on the beautiful waterways and narrow fiords of southeastern Alaska may pass through an unmarred landscape.

Every year more gravel and other material from the tidelands are needed for highway construction and similar developments. How this demand can be met efficiently and economically without unnecessary damage or destruction to other resource values is a problem of growing concern in the Division of Lands. When the materials are taken in large quantities, serious erosion of the uplands frequently occurs. Scenic, recreational, and historical values can be lost and important fisheries may be harmed. The difficulty is accentuated in that tidal areas containing the most desirable materials for construction purposes often are the same areas that are most valuable for other resource uses, and it has become particularly acute in southeast Alaska where there are few sources of gravel other than in those intertidal zones around the mouths of the rivers which are also important salmon spawning areas. There is need for a statewide inventory to determine those areas where the removal of materials will not conflict appreciably with other resources, and for scientific and engineering research to identify methods of removal that will minimize losses of these other values. The 1964 earthquake which caused such untold damage to many tideland areas, especially along the coast of southcentral Alaska, has created a need for further research, for the processes of coastal and shore erosion—normally occurring over many decades—have been compressed into a very short period of time. The Department of Fish and Game, desirous of protecting important wildlife and fishery values, recently established a new position of "water coordinator" to review all leases and other applications to the state requesting permission to remove sand and gravel or otherwise disturb creeks, rivers, and tidelands. However, until much greater information is available about the tidelands and the natural and man-made influences on them, it will be difficult to establish equitable standards and leasing regulations for their use and protection.

This brief review of a number of conflicts in land and resource use reveals one point clearly. If Alaska is to maximize economic benefits from its magnificent resource endowment without destroying the land's distinctive values, many matters require careful research. What the state needs now more than anything else is more precise and better integrated knowledge about the northern environment and related problems of land management and development. As an example, to guide its selection, classification, and disposal programs the state sorely needs detailed area-by-area resource surveys of the kind discussed and recommended by the Conservation Foundation is its report to the Secretary of the

Interior in 1952. Had the Interior Department begun such resource inventories at that time, the state land program today could be carried forward with the guidance of sound factual knowledge rather than in a hit-or-miss manner which can lead to unnecessary economic and social costs and burdensome land management problems for both the state and federal government in the years ahead.

Much of this research can only be accomplished by the various government agencies because of the nature of the tasks, but there are other avenues that should be pursued concurrently. Consideration should be given, for instance, to the possibility of establishing a northern wildland research and resource management center at the University of Alaska to conduct a continuous program of basic scientific research. The University is ideally suited for this purpose because of its far northern location and the array of scientific staff and research facilities already established there. These include an Institute of Arctic Biology, the Alaska Cooperative Wildlife Research Unit, a Northern Forest Experiment Station, a Mineral Industry Research Laboratory, the Geophysical Institute, the Institute of Economic, Social, and Government Research, the Institute of Marine Sciences, a Federal Water Pollution Laboratory, the Naval Arctic Research Laboratory at Point Barrow, and the offices, laboratories, and research facilities of numerous state and federal resource agencies. The wildlands in northern Alaska provide an unparalleled opportunity for establishing large and varied study plots on both state and federal lands, and only a few hundred miles north of the University lies the 9-million-acre Arctic National Wildlife Range with outstanding potential for scientific research. A permanent cooperative program, sponsored by state and federal governments, by private foundations, and by interested industrial organizations, for research and graduate education in multiple land-use planning, wildland and wilderness management, and studies of socio-economic and ecological relationships in land management, would be invaluable not only to Alaska but to many other undeveloped regions throughout the world where increasing populations, rising demands upon natural resources, and rapidly expanding technologies indicate the probability of far-reaching environmental changes in the years ahead. Alaska offers an excellent outdoor research laboratory for these purposes.

It is obvious that the state government is in no position to conduct much of the research now needed in Alaska. In the first place, the state's poor financial position precludes any large expenditures for this purpose. In the second place, many of the complex policy issues demanding research are highly controversial, and no one agency or level of government is in a position to take an altogether objective view. A privately sponsored program that transcends the partisanship of party and special interest group, and that is free to disseminate the findings to the policy makers and the people of Alaska, can best meet the need for objective research to clarify specific problems, to formulate alternatives, to analyze consequences, and to present policy recommendations based on reasoned conclusions, leaving the final decisions to those charged with responsibility and accountability. A number of large private foundations have been fully apprised of this situation, and various proposals have been submitted over the years in an effort to gain their support in a cooperative state, federal, and private program to carry out research aimed squarely at these vital policy issues; but so far the response has been negative. Ironically, millions and millions of dollars are made available each year throughout the United States by these organizations for programs designed to correct past errors of public policy, or to moderate their impact, but a deaf ear is turned to Alaska in its search for modest financial aid to embark upon a research program aimed at preventing the same mistakes from occurring.

Chapter 8

Interagency and Jurisdictional Conflicts

THE authority to classify land for its highest use before disposing of it has long been recognized as an indispensable tool of government in encouraging the development of meaningful patterns of land settlement and resource use, and most land management agencies at both the federal and state levels have long operated with this power. One glaring exception has been the Bureau of Land Management, the agency charged with managing by far the largest acreage of public land in the United States—the unreserved and unappropriated federal public domain. With passage of the Taylor Grazing Act in 1934 (48 U.S. Stat., 1296), the Bureau was finally given the power to classify the remaining lands under its jurisdiction in the western states, but the provisions of this act were not extended to Alaska. Consequently, the entire 270 million acres of public domain lands—encompassing nearly three-quarters of the total area of the state—have been open to private entry and settlement without the protection assured by modern techniques of land classification. From the swamps to the mountains, all these lands have been subject to the indiscriminate filing of private claims under the federal land laws, and over the years thousands of acres of nonagricultural lands were taken up under the homestead law because there was no legal means to prevent such settlement. The Bureau of Land Management has reported instances of 70 percent slopes being put to cultivation and exposed to heavy erosion damage by homesteaders who, for the most part, never intended to farm the land once title was gained, but sought it for other resource values or for speculative purposes. It is true that many of these claims eventually failed before patent was obtained, but in the interim the land was unavailable for other perhaps more appropriate uses, and in many cases suffered considerably from efforts by the settlers to prove their claims.

This lack of classification authority has not only created extremely difficult problems for the Bureau in carrying out its land management functions in Alaska, but it has also forced the state Division of Lands to make what may be termed "defensive" land selections—costly and untimely selections which have been required to prevent haphazard private land developments and scattered settlement on the federal public domain. Otherwise such sporadic development could saddle the state with impossible financial burdens in providing roads, schools, and other public services demanded by the settlers, or result in the destruction of lands and resources whose high potential value for other uses might have led the state to select them in the future. A good example is the filing of federal homesteads on public domain lands having birch stands that undoubtedly will be of great commercial value in the years ahead. If this valuable timber land is broken up into small homestead parcels, the prospects for developing an important industry on the basis of this resource will be poor. Thus, the state is being forced to select these lands prematurely to prevent such a pattern of land ownership from developing. Since the resource is not of immediate commercial value, the state could have waited ten or more years before making selections had the Bureau of Land Management been able to classify these lands to prevent indiscriminate homesteading. Over the years many prime public recreation areas have also been lost in this fashion owing to the inability of the federal agency to act.

Passage by Congress in 1964 of the Classification and Multiple-Use Act (Public Law 88–607) can do much to alleviate this problem, for it provides the Bureau of Land Management with a positive mandate to classify, and manage for multiple use, all remaining public domain lands in the United States, including those in Alaska. Since this is basically the same authority under which the state now operates, it opens the way for more meaningful federal-state cooperation in land management, and should reduce the need for "defensive" land selections by the state. Planning of a program to carry out the intent of this legislation has begun, and in the years ahead the Bureau of Land Management may at last be able to live up to its name. Moreover Congress has established the Public Land Law Review Commission (88–606) to conduct a detailed and comprehensive examination during a four-year period of all federal land laws, regulations, and policies, and to make recommendation to the President and Congress for necessary changes. Since well over half of all federal lands are located in Alaska, the state has a large stake in the outcome of this study. Hopefully, it will result in the creation of a modernized system of federal land laws that will insure maximum benefits to all the people from the public lands. Wholesale revision is long overdue.

Another area of conflict between the Bureau of Land Management and the state Division of Lands has arisen recently as a result of the pattern of state land selections. Since the Division has the prerogative to make its selections anywhere on the public domain, the Bureau has been reluctant to undertake development work for recreation, timber inventory, access roads, or other purposes because such investments merely increase the land value and, therefore, the likelihood that the state will select those lands. The Bureau also fears that the state's tendency in the last two years to make small "spot" selections in order to obtain only those lands of highest immediate value will result in a pattern of scattered and mixed federal-state land ownership that eventually will prove as costly and unmanageable for both units of government as the checkerboard pattern that was created in the West by the earlier in-place land grants. The Bureau has taken the attitude that the state of Alaska should follow a definite pattern of land selection designed to block out meaningful management units, and that this knowledge should be made available to the Bureau in order that it may carry out work on other public lands without fear of indiscriminate state selection, at least for a given period of time. The Bureau is not for instance likely to spend money on the construction of public access roads to open resources and recreation areas on public domain lands unless it knows which areas are most likely to remain in federal ownership for some reasonable period of time.

Until the two levels of government can reach much closer agreement on this issue, Alaska will continue to suffer a major loss in federal investment on the public domain. In recent months they have moved toward more meaningful coordination of selection and management programs, and both agencies hold great hopes for future progress. The new Classification and Multiple-Use Act makes this a real possibility.

Policy conflicts between the state and the United States Forest Service have hindered the selection from the national forests of the 400,000 acre land grant allowed in the Statehood Act for the purposes of community development and expansion. So far, less than 10,000 acres have been selected, and very little of that has received approval from the Secretary of Agriculture. This approval is necessary under the terms of the Statehood Act; it gives the Forest Service, in contrast to the position of the Bureau of Land Management, the power to exercise a strong control over the pattern of state selections on national forest lands. The Forest Service has devised definite criteria to guide state selections, and according to its interpretation of the intent of the community grant, the lands to be selected must be "either adjacent to established communities or suitable for prospective community centers or recreation areas."[1] In all cases, the state is required to submit adequate data to substantiate the need for the land. If the selection is for a prospective community, the state must be able to provide a reasonable assurance, based on the probability of new industry or other reasonable prospective developments, that a

1. U.S. Forest Service, "Manual," Title 5400, pp. 142–48.

community will be established, and the amount of land selected must be limited to an area that the community could reasonably be expected to use in the foreseeable future. Selections for community recreation purposes must be within or near an established or prospective community, and since the primary purpose is to meet the needs for municipal parks, playgrounds, or civic centers, the Forest Service requires that the land must be readily accessible to all of the people in the community. Before approving a grant it may also require an easement from the state for rights-of-way, or set other restrictions considered necessary to develop and protect the national forest resources and to insure their efficient management.

It has been the state's contention that these selection requirements are much too stringent and that the Forest Service has misinterpreted the intent of the law. Under these terms the state contends it will never be able to select more than a very small portion of the total community grant during the twenty-five year period allotted. Yet the Forest Service fears that if the community grant provision is interpreted too loosely, the state might select lands in such a manner as to disrupt completely the long-range plans for multiple-use management which it has been developing for the forests of Alaska over the last ten years. A court case may be necessary some time in the future to resolve this conflict. The issue emphasizes the need for greater mutual understanding and cooperation between the two levels of government, for only through such cooperative planning will it be possible to arrive at a rational pattern of land use which will serve the state's long-range interests in community development and at the same time meet the needs for national forest management and protection. Several meetings were held recently between representatives of the Forest Service and the Division of Lands, and some progress is being made in the selection and processing of lands even though they still disagree on the extent to which the state must substantiate its need for proposed selections.

Controversy over the current timber export policies of both state and federal agencies indicates the need for a closer examination of the issues involved. Early in the century the Forest Service prohibited the export of round logs from Alaska, hoping thus to encourage the establishment of milling and processing facilities. Without some regulation, the Service feared, the timber from the national forests in Alaska would be logged and shipped to the Pacific Northwest, to the detriment of the economy of the territory. The regulations required that timber cut from these national forests should be processed, or receive at least some stages of primary manufacture, before being shipped out of the territory, and, except for minor modifications, they remain in effect today. The Bureau of Land Management adopted a similar though somewhat more flexible policy with respect to harvesting the vast forest lands in interior Alaska; and shortly after statehood, the government of Alaska also promulgated a non-export policy for state forests, although the state does permit some export of minor species, defined to include cedar, birch, and cottonwood, under certain circumstances. The major species of Sitka spruce, western hemlock, and white spruce cannot be exported except under special circumstances for limited periods.

While it is generally conceded that the Forest Service's non-export policy may have been instrumental in the eventual construction of two pulp mills in southeastern Alaska in the 1950's, many have been concerned about the logic of applying this policy to the interior forest lands which the state is now in the process of selecting. Under present economic conditions, it is argued, these far northern forests are marginal, and unless the non-export policy is relaxed it will be many decades before this renewable natural resource can be utilized. Proponents of this view regard logging as another basic industry, no different from the extractive mining industry, that could contribute importantly to the interior economy through increased payrolls and associated services. They point out that a basic tool of timber management is harvest, and that protection of forests from fire and other destructive agents cannot long be justified financially by the state if the forests are not put to use. They note that access roads financed by timber removal would open the way for development of other resources such as mining, agriculture, and recreation. They also emphasize that the Alaska Constitution provides for the management of forest lands on a sustained yield basis, and in meeting this requirement no more timber could be cut than would be replaced through regeneration, regardless of the market for timber. Currently far less than one percent of the allowable harvest is being cut on interior forest lands, and these proponents believe the resulting increased age of the timber stands is not only unhealthy and uneconomic, but also results in the loss of large quantities of otherwise merchantable timber each year through deterioration and decay. They believe processing industries will be started in the interior when it becomes economically feasible, and that in the meantime controlled harvesting for export would benefit both forest and economy.

Conversely, there are those who believe a relaxation of the present non-export policy would have exactly the opposite effect on the future economy, and would also adversely influence existing forest industries. The two pulp mills, they point out, have invested heavily in Alaska despite the high costs of labor and construction. If "outside" competitors are allowed to purchase round logs and export them to low-cost areas for processing, the cost of logs at the Alaska mills will necessarily increase, thus reducing the margin of profit of these established local industries, which is already at the lower limits. Proponents of this view believe the present non-export policy of the Forest Service is not only a primary factor in the development of a large timber processing industry in southeastern Alaska but that the policy will effect identical results throughout the state. And they have called attention to recent studies of underdeveloped countries throughout the world which indicate that nations attempting to develop an economy based on the extraction and export of raw resources are doomed to fall farther behind manufacturing nations in the level of living. The non-export timber policy, they assert, will help to prevent this from happening in Alaska.

In no other state has this non-export policy been carried to the extreme it has in Alaska. The state's two closest neighbors, British

Columbia and Washington, are large exporters of round logs, with no apparent damage to the development of local processing industries. This is not a simple black or white issue, and what is now needed is an objective economic analysis of the various alternatives and their long-range consequences so that policy-makers can arrive at decisions on the basis of facts instead of prevailing opinion and unsupported judgments. How far is the state prepared to go in controlling exports in this manner? If the policy is good for the developing timber industry, then why not also apply it to other natural resources? These questions are of major importance to the Alaska economy, for Japan may possibly provide a large permanent export market not only for timber from interior forests but for other raw materials as well, if a mutually advantageous policy can be attained.

The creation of new units of government, the boroughs, has brought in its wake yet another series of problems for the state's land program. The territory of Alaska had no units of government between the states and the cities, and instead of creating counties on the pattern of most other states, the Constitution and the state legislature provided for the establishment of an altogether original and more streamlined intermediate form of government designed to meet the peculiar physical and socio-economic conditions of the state. The boroughs are only now coming into existence. At the present time there are nine of them, and they encompass relatively large land areas around the main centers of population, as may be noted in Map 3. Altogether they cover nearly 40 million acres, or an area slightly larger than the state of Michigan; they contain over 80 percent of the total population of the state, including military personnel, and nearly all economic development is occurring within their boundaries. Because of their wide powers, the boroughs are destined to become extremely important political units in the years ahead.

The state legislature passed an act in 1963 allowing each organized borough to select 10 percent of the "vacant unappropriated, unreserved state lands" within its boundaries (52 SLA 1963). This has been defined to mean those state lands "classified by the state as available for disposal" within the borough boundaries, which includes lands classified as agricultural, commercial-industrial, private recreational, residential, utility, and watershed lands. Not available for selection by the borough are all tide and submerged lands regardless of their classification; any lands classified as grazing, timber, public recreation, material, mineral or reserved use, and all university, mental health, and school lands. All mineral rights are also retained by the state. Thus, by its classification authority, the state is in a position to determine in large measure the location and amount of land available for selection by the boroughs. (These borough selections can be made within five years after state lands in the borough become available, and since the statehood land grant provides for state selections over a period of twenty-five years, borough selections will continue throughout the same period and for five years thereafter.)

The legislature anticipated that these land selections would serve two related purposes: to act as an incentive for the establishment of boroughs and the voluntary expansion of their functions leading toward greater responsibility for local self-government; and to provide financial assistance for these new units of government which, for the most part, will be hard pressed for operating capital during the formative years. As the author of the bill expressed it:

> the borough assembly should have some hand in the utilization of natural resources in its own area. Ten percent is only a minimum grant. As soon as some experience is gained by boroughs, I hope that additional lands, as well as portions of other resources, are turned over to the borough for utilization. It is hoped that all functions of a local nature will ultimately be handled by the boroughs and cities. The state can make continuing grants to the borough for all functions which the borough assumes and which it takes over from the state. In this way, there will be no penalty imposed on those who take the initiative and seize self-government, as contrasted with those who continually look to the state for long distance care, guidance and sustenance.[2]

2. Representative John Rader, "An Explanation of Bill for the Incorporation of First Class Organized Boroughs," 1963 (mimeo), pp. 6–7.

While there is no denying the importance of establishing viable units of government at this intermediate level, there is serious doubt as to the efficacy of using land grants from the state as a financial incentive. The boroughs naturally will need to acquire a certain amount of land over the years for schools and other building sites, equipment yards, community expansion, recreation areas, watershed protection, new townsites, and various other public purposes, and it is logical that means should be provided to meet these needs as efficiently as possible from the state land patrimony. The State Land Act already provides authority for the Division of Lands to grant such lands to municipalities and other local governmental units at less than the appraised value. Since 1958, the Division of Lands has leased or sold over 20,000 acres of land to the units of government at a minimum cost. However, to place these local units of government in the business of land management and disposal in competition with the state agency is another matter. It represents an illogical fracturing of governmental responsibility, and could actually hamper the development of the boroughs and eventually undermine the entire state land program.

Contrary to popular belief, there is no such thing as "free" land. As is well illustrated by the state's own experience, it costs money not only to select each acre of land but also to provide the protection and management required if the land is to become an asset rather than a liability. The principal economic value of land lies not in the direct revenues gained from its disposal but rather in the increased capital investment, employment, and tax base resulting from the lands and resources being put into production. If selections by the boroughs are aimed at maximizing their direct revenues by immediate disposal, land units otherwise suitable for large-scale management might be easily lost in a fractured pattern of land ownership. It is unreasonable to expect that a large number of local governmental units could do the job anywhere near as effectively and efficiently as the state government.

Since the borough land selection legislation has been in effect only a short time, it is too early to determine what the full implications may be. The potential seriousness of the problem has however been heightened by recent proposals presented to the state legislature aimed at increasing the percentage of state lands that can be selected by the boroughs, including tide and submerged lands, and providing similar land grants to cities and towns. There is urgent need for a thorough examination of this philosophy before it is carried any further. Unnecessary conflict and antagonism between the state and the boroughs could be avoided by policies that allow these two levels of government to cooperate toward mutually desirable ends.

A system, for example, in which development is jointly planned but the state maintains ownership and management while sharing land and resource revenues with the boroughs would undoubtedly prove much more advantageous to both. Something on this order appears to be evolving. Many of the boroughs do not have the financial ability or the manpower at the present time to initiate and maintain an efficient land management program, and, as a result, the 1965 State Legislature made provision (100 SLA 1965) for the boroughs to enter into an agreement with the state of Alaska to have the Division of Lands manage their selections. Three of the nine boroughs have already done this, and it is very likely that most of the others will do likewise. Under these agreements the state not only provides such services as management, protection, surveying, and classification of the lands at cost, but also handles all leases, sales, or other disposals of borough lands and resources with the approval of the borough assembly. To preserve the integrity of grazing and timber management units, the existing agreements stipulate that grazing and timber lands selected by the boroughs will remain under the direct management of the state. The boroughs reap the revenues, but cannot sell or in any way dispose of these two classes of land. These management agreements help to promote close cooperation in land planning and management between the two levels of government. They also indicate that the boroughs are beginning to realize both the costs and the heavy responsibilities that ownership of public land entails, and that they are willing to take a more cautious and rational approach to the future after the early jubilance of finding themselves in the real estate business. It is fitting that these intermediate units of government should assume responsibility for the proper development of lands whose value is chiefly for local use—for residential, commercial, and industrial purposes, for private and public recreation and enjoyment. But if the boroughs move into the land business on a grandiose scale to raise revenue, the state land program will certainly be in jeopardy. The quality of the landscape around the major cities and towns will be determined largely by the way these units of government understand their prerogatives. Alaska could avoid many of the deplorable problems of environmental decay now tormenting most urban and metropolitan areas in the United States, if the boroughs are not hamstrung from the beginning by ill-advised legislation and actions based on erroneous assumptions.[3]

All levels of government in Alaska are seeing changes and innovations, and the state is in a favorable position to develop a new and original approach to government cooperation in land use and development. Only time will tell whether the people of the region can rise to the challenge.

3. All land outside the organized boroughs is included in one vast "unorganized borough" for which the state legislature must provide schools, health facilities, and other local services. It is possible, and probably desirable, that the legislature should consider special zoning legislation for this area. In the 1965 session of the Alaska State Legislature a proposal was made, but not passed, that zoning regulations for all lands outside the organized boroughs should be prepared and administered by the Division of Lands. Such legislation is needed for another reason. The recent Public Land Sale Act (P.L. 88–608), designed to bring federal land use into harmony with local needs where possible, provides that local units of government can purchase at low cost certain federal lands within their boundaries if adequate planning and zoning regulations have been enacted. The nine organized boroughs can qualify under the provisions of this act since they already have the authority and have begun to establish comprehensive planning and zoning regulations, but the vast remaining area of Alaska in the so-called unorganized borough so far has been given no such power.

Chapter 9

Planning and the Political Struggle

LAND policy is ubiquitous. It touches and permeates many other important areas of public policy which in turn exert influence on land policy. Decisions for the selection, management, and disposal of lands are vital to the state's future, and intelligent programming during the next two decades hinges upon greater knowledge than now exists of the location, quantity, and quality of natural resources and a much closer integration of the programs of many different local, state and federal agencies. The Division of Lands is to be highly commended for the quality of the program it has launched and carried forward during the first critical years of statehood, but it can be severely hamstrung. In substance, if the state land patrimony is to make its fullest contribution to the social and economic well-being of the people of Alaska there must be a much greater emphasis on long-range statewide planning in the years ahead. Planning is no luxury, but a necessity, and its lack has been sorely felt in Alaska on both the state and federal levels.

In the first comprehensive study of Alaska's development possibilities in 1937, the National Resources Committee was appalled at the lack of essential information about the region's lands and resources and the absence of coordination among the numerous federal resource agencies with major responsibilities in Alaska. The Committee recommended greatly enlarged programs of land surveying and mapping, resource inventories, land classification, mineral exploration, and many other scientific investigations to fill the wide gaps in existing knowledge; and it recommended the establishment of a permanent Alaska planning agency to prepare a long-range integrated plan for the region. The Committee concluded that "a national policy or plan for Alaska ought not to vacillate with the shifting winds of politics. It should be altered only as broad trends in technology indicate the need of alteration or as national social aspirations undergo substantial change."[1] These recommendations went unheeded, and national policy toward Alaska continued to drift. Though many similar recommendations were made over the years by various public and private study groups, the situation changed very little. Some formal cooperation among agencies within the Department of the Interior has been possible since 1948 through the creation of the Alaska Field Committee consisting of ranking representatives of its bureaus in Alaska and a chairman appointed by, and responsible to, the Secretary of the Interior. This was a step in the right direction but the Committee's jurisdiction is limited to Interior agencies, and it has no authority to coordinate the field programs of the various bureaus within the Department.

Efforts have been made by the state to establish a planning agency but the results have also been ineffectual. Shortly after statehood, a Division of Planning with broad powers was created and installed in the Office of the Governor. With the full support of the chief executive, the agency began the difficult task of preparing a long-range comprehensive development plan for the whole of Alaska, and had made useful progress when in 1962 a private consulting firm, Arthur D. Little, Inc., of Boston, was invited by the state legislature to conduct a series of resource studies and advise the state on problems of economic development. Among its proposals, the firm recommended that a new Department of Economic Development should be established, and that the planning function should be transferred from the

1. National Resources Committee, *Alaska: Its Resources and Development* (Washington: Govt. Printing Office, 1937), p. 29.

Governor's Office to the new department. Had the consulting firm taken the time to study the sad history of state planning under similar situations throughout the United States, it might have recognized the fallacy of this approach. But the recommendation was adopted, and during the next few years state planning languished as a division attached to a line agency whose primary function centered on "selling Alaska" to out-of-state industrialists and potential investors, tourist promotion, national advertising, and the like. Late in 1965, the planning agency was again moved back into the Office of the Governor, a fact which gave some indication that the state had recognized its earlier decision to be an unfortunate misconception of the role of planning and its place in the governmental hierarchy.

The situation existing on national forest lands offers a vivid illustration of the need for a formal mechanism to coordinate resource programs among federal and state agencies. Periodic reference was made in the last chapter to the Forest Service's multiple use plan which has been in the development stage for at least ten years. An excellent manual has been prepared setting out management policies and criteria to be used in guiding the decisions of those in the agency charged with drawing up the actual plans in the various subregions of these two national forests. It is a clear, concise document establishing a basic framework for reconciling those conflicts between different resource uses that are normally encountered in multiple use planning. Unlike nearly all other federal or state resource agencies, the Forest Service has managed to obtain both funds and professional staff for the job, and multiple land use planning in the national forests is much further advanced than elsewhere in Alaska.

Unfortunately, however, there are flaws marring the excellence of these efforts. The Forest Service has been less than enthusiastic about coordinating its plans and programs with other resource agencies which also have important functions in the national forests. In planning the selection and classification of important water influence zones and prime wildlife habitat zones, for instance, little effort has been made to enlist the help of the Department of Fish and Game, even though the Department has a vital interest in the protection and management of both the commercial fisheries and the sport fish and wildlife resources in the national forests. Nor have the people of the region been drawn into the planning process even though nearly half of the state's population is located in or very close to the national forests. Probably less than five percent of this population is aware that decisions are being made that will affect their welfare for decades to come. There are no public hearings; no local advisory councils; no formal mechanism for review. Such bureau autonomy cannot be tolerated in the field of natural resources where physical, economic, and social interrelations are both extremely complex and critically important to the future of the state. The situation desperately demands joint planning involving all levels of government.

Ironically, hope is emerging from disaster. Shortly after the earthquake struck in March, 1964, President Johnson established an emergency Federal Reconstruction and Development Planning Commission for Alaska which dealt forcefully and efficiently with the many problems created by the quake. Chaired by Senator Clinton P. Anderson, the Commission consisted of cabinet members and other Washington officials whose departments or agencies had important functions in Alaska. A state counterpart was formed by the governor to work closely with the federal commission. By September, 1964, reconstruction was completed, and in its final report the Federal Reconstruction Commission recommended the establishment of a permanent joint federal-state committee to conduct a program of long-range economic and resource development planning in Alaska. "This long-range planning," the report concluded, "should move forward at once, building upon the momentum developed in the course of reconstruction." [2] A few weeks later President Johnson signed Execu-

2. Federal Reconstruction and Development Planning Commission for Alaska, *Response to Disaster* (Washington: Govt. Printing Office, September 1964), p. 38.

tive Order No. 11182, establishing a unique federal organizational mechanism to carry out this recommendation. Two reasons were listed to justify the need:

(1) the Federal Government and the State of Alaska continue to have a common interest in assuring the most effective use of Federal and State programs and funds in advancing the long-range progress of the state; and
(2) such effective use is dependent upon coordination of Federal and State programs which affect the general economic development of the State and the long-range conservation and use of its natural resources, and upon cooperative Federal and State effort with respect to the planning of such programs.

Actually the roots of this important executive order reach back much further than the earthquake. During his campaign for the United States Presidency in 1960, John F. Kennedy delivered a speech on the floor of the Senate in which he said:

We must meet the challenge of Alaska. . . . One of the first tasks . . . must be to develop a complete blueprint for Alaskan resource development . . . Such a plan would allow for a coordinated development of all of Alaska's resources. . . .

We must be careful to avoid the same piecemeal, uncoordinated, wasteful approach which has too often characterized our resource development in the past.[3]

Following the election, the Alaska governor and congressional delegation proposed to President Kennedy the establishment of an Alaska Development Commission to accomplish these purposes. In a lengthy letter to the President in October, 1962, they suggested the Commission be composed of representatives of federal and state agencies which have a substantial interest in the development of Alaska.

The commission should have at its head an independent chairman, appointed by the President in order that all commission efforts be properly integrated. To accomplish this, the commission chairman should be empowered to appoint an executive staff responsible to him. . . . We believe firmly in the use of an executive order for this purpose because of its expedition and flexibility in meeting the immediate need.[4]

3. Speech on the floor of the U.S. Senate, June 24, 1960.

4. Letter to President Kennedy, dated October 17, 1962 (circulated in mimeo by State of Alaska, Office of the Governor).

The President indicated his agreement, and the proposed organization was on the point of receiving formal authorization when President Kennedy was assassinated. In the months immediately following, it was hardly a matter of national priority, and only with the earthquake of March 27 did it again come into focus. Then the language of the earlier proposed executive order was quickly adopted and became the basis for President Johnson's executive orders establishing both the emergency Reconstruction Commission as well as the more recent permanent Development Planning Committee for Alaska. One of the main points to be noted is the active role of the state government in bringing about the establishment of this joint federal-state planning organization. This is extremely important for without the full cooperation of the state in the planning process the program will languish and die.

Two permanent committees were established by the recent executive order. A President's Review Committee for Development Planning provides general direction and guidance from Washington, D.C., while the responsibility for actually developing coordinated plans is carried out in Alaska by a Federal Field Committee for Development Planning.

The Review Committee is composed of the following officials: the Secretary of Commerce (chairman), the Secretaries of the Interior, of Agriculture, of Labor, of Defense, and the Secretary of Health, Education, and Welfare; the Administrators of the Housing and Home Finance Agency, of the Small Business Administration, and of the Federal Aviation Agency; the Chairman of the Public Power Commission; and two public members appointed by the President. The Field Committee consists of a chairman appointed by the President, ten members designated by and representing the officers on the Review Committee, and two public members appointed by the President. Its chairman may also request other federal agencies to name a representative when matters of substantial interest require their participation.

The Field Committee serves as the principal instrumentality for developing coordinated plans for all federal programs which contribute to economic and resource development in Alaska, and for recommending appropriate action by the federal government to carry out such plans. The executive order directs the Field Committee to cooperate with the state of Alaska in surveys and studies which will provide the information necessary for economic and resources development in Alaska, and in drawing up plans, in conjunction with federal, state, and local agencies, which will ensure the most effective allocation of available funds. It is also to cooperate in preparing legislative and other recommendations for both short- and long-range governmental programs. Presumably, the state of Alaska will create a counterpart organization to work with the federal committees.

The chairman of the Federal Field Committee is authorized to establish subcommittees as may be necessary and to employ personnel required to carry out activities of the Field Committee. All developmental programs will be conducted by the respective agencies. Tentative plans and recommendations prepared by the Field Committee are to be transmitted for review and comment to the governor of Alaska, to heads of interested federal agencies, and to the Review Committee in Washington, D.C. When final plans have been perfected and confirmed, they will be transmitted by the Review Committee directly to the President of the United States for his consideration and approval. Never before has a state of the Union been given such an excellent opportunity to formulate and carry out joint plans with the federal government on the level envisioned in this executive order. It is an altogether new organizational technique providing direct access to the highest levels of policy making in the federal hierarchy, and the normal budgetary process should be greatly simplified and expedited for those agency and departmental programs which are approved and incorporated in the unified plans.

Early in 1965 the two federal committees were brought into active operation. The chairman and public members were appointed by the President, and the Field Committee for Development Planning met and immediately prepared the ground by hiring staff and by designating subcommittees and task forces, composed of officials from both federal and state agencies, to prepare joint background reports with recommendations for action in each of the major resource fields. For the first time in Alaska's history, the many federal and state resource agencies are discussing their conflicts and mutual problems, and attempting to coordinate their varied programs toward common goals in the public interest.

While this organizational mechanism is sufficiently new and different to warrant some optimism, many obstacles and impediments lie in the way of fulfillment of the intent of the executive order. It is naive to believe that a stroke of the Presidential pen is sufficient to obtain meaningful cooperation among competing bureaucracies. Such coordination is extremely difficult to attain, as the history of agency relations in river basin development in this country attests. During the past thirty years a number of interagency coordinating committees have been established to bring together both federal and state personnel dealing with resource problems, and their failure has been well documented in a substantial number of books and articles which have laid bare the pervasive and far-reaching character of the bureaucratic struggle.

In reviewing this history, the political scientist Norman Wengert concluded that committees of equals, seeking by negotiation, discussion, and bargaining to work out conflicts and disagreements normally produce results which are never greater than the imagination of the least of the participants, never broader than the legal powers of each member, and usually only as significant as the lowest common denominator. He noted that although agreement is a desirable goal of coordination, a realistic analysis of coordination processes reveals that effective administration often requires decisions against the interests of some and favorable to the interests of others. Organizational arrangements which only deal with areas of agreement, which ignore conflicts and refuse to face up to consequences, are not adequate to the task of resource administration.[5] In summarizing the many different conflicts and struggles over resource policy, he concluded:

Often the most passionate [struggle] has been that among scientists and experts concerned with resource technology, for the unity of expert opinion which early conservationists envisioned has just not materialized. Partly a consequence of specialization and partly a reflection of biases and valuation conflicts, the struggle among experts most frequently is evidenced in the effort of competing bureaucracies to carry through their particular views of sound policy. Except for half hearted and generally abortive attempts to provide mechanisms for coordination, the conflicts among technicians remain one of the most complex aspects of current resource policy.[6]

It remains to be seen whether the Alaska experiment in joint federal-state planning will be able to overcome these inherent weaknesses. Success hinges on many factors: the extent of the powers given the chairman, and his ability to use them in resolving conflicts and shaping a sound planning program (it would be tragic, for example, if the program became oriented primarily toward industrial promotion, or was seen as a pork barrel mechanism to gain local development at the expense of the national treasury); the character of the leadership and support provided by the President and his Review Committee for Development Planning; the attitudes of the participants representing the various agencies and departments at both the Washington and the field levels; the reaction of Congress to this new coordinative technique; how the state government proceeds in establishing a comparable body; and the degree of political support it receives from the governor, the legislature, and the people of Alaska.

Alaska's lands and resources can play a highly significant role in the nation's future, but the necessary preparations must be made now if the state is to benefit from rather than be overwhelmed by the march of events, for the difficulties are as great

5. Norman Wengert, *Natural Resources and the Political Struggle* (New York: Doubleday & Co., 1955), p. 46.
6. *Ibid.*, p. 23.

as the possibilities are exciting. Planning is no philosopher's stone providing answers to all policy issues, but if properly integrated in the political process it can become instrumental in the shaping of a pleasing and productive environment worthy of man. Nothing is more to be wished, welcomed, and urged.

Chapter 10

A Conservation Ethic

LAND is a commodity altogether different from what it was a century ago. Space itself is rapidly becoming a natural resource to be protected and conserved rather than an obstacle to be overcome. In a recent article dealing with the nation's rapid population growth, John D. Rockefeller III wrote:

> Consider our land itself. It stretched before the eyes of our forefathers in vast, unexplored reaches. The wealth of its resources was unimaginable, its westward horizons unlimited. Once we beckoned immigrants to help us settle the land. The Northwest Ordinance and the Homestead Act were milestones of national policy designed to put lands in the hands of the people. Today we hold back the immigrants while we strive for a broader policy of conservation. We seek not to sell land to the people, but to protect it. Today we treasure the remaining stretch of lovely beach and the still virgin forest. The land has filled up, the unlimited was found to have a limit, and the infinite distances to be finite indeed.[1]

This changing concept of land—the growing emphasis on the esthetics of land use—has deep and far-reaching implications, and it is important that Alaska's future be conceived, her lands and resources weighed, in the perspective of a new national vision.

The esthetics of land use is not simply a matter of preserving scenic and recreation lands or protecting wildlife resources so they can be viewed and enjoyed by the public. These are, of

1. John D. Rockefeller III., "The Hidden Crisis," *Look Magazine,* February 9, 1965, p. 79.

course, essential parts of the whole, but it is no more possible to separate them from other contemporary problems of the quality of the environment than it is to segregate America from the rest of the world. Esthetic enjoyment is a highly subjective matter, but the esthetic experience involves simultaneously all the senses of man—sight, smell, hearing, touch, and taste. If four of these senses are being gratified but one is being rudely offended, then enjoyment is impaired and degraded. The scenic beauty of a mountain landscape can be obliterated by the foul odors emitted from a pulp mill; the enjoyment of a trip to a park can be cancelled if all the access routes to it are crowded with honky-tonks, hamburger stands, billboards, and other cheap commercial developments. Clearly a concern for the esthetics of land use must encompass all forms of environmental pollution, must be a concern for the quality of the total environment—both natural and man-made—and how man influences and is influenced by it.

Not long ago a *New York Times* editorial pointed out that beauty has been a pantywaist word in this country until very recently.[2] But today, in the mid-1960's, beauty has suddenly become a major national issue requiring special and immediate attention. This is the "quiet crisis" that Secretary of the Interior Stewart Udall was referring to when he wrote about the paradox of American society which today stands poised on a pinnacle of wealth and power, but whose environmental standard has steadily declined, so that we live in a land blighted by noise and pollution, a land of vanishing beauty, of increasing ugliness, of shrinking open space. "We cannot afford an America," he said, "where expedience tramples upon esthetics, and development decisions are made with an eye only on the present."[3]

Similar concern has been voiced by scholars, politicians, and citizens across the country, and a giant step towards a solution has been made by President Johnson, when he declared the preservation of natural beauty a primary tenet in his program for the

2. *New York Times,* December 10, 1964.

3. Stewart Udall, *The Quiet Crisis* (New York: Holt, Rinehart and Winston, 1963), p. 190.

Great Society. In February, 1965, shortly after his inauguration, he presented an historic message to Congress calling for a massive public effort to rescue our cities and the countryside from blight. Said the President:

> The increasing tempo of urbanization and growth is already depriving many Americans of the right to live in decent surroundings. More of our people are crowded into cities and being cut off from nature. Cities themselves reach out into the countryside, destroying streams and trees and meadows as they go. A modern highway may wipe out the equivalent of a fifty acre park with every mile. And people move out from the city to get closer to nature only to find that nature has moved farther from them.
>
> The modern technology, which has added much to our lives can also have a darker side. Its uncontrolled waste products are menacing the world we live in, our enjoyment and our health. The air we breathe, our water, our soil and wildlife, are being blighted by the poisons and chemicals which are the by-products of technology and industry. The skeletons of discarded cars litter the countryside. The same society which receives the rewards of technology, must, as a cooperating whole, take responsibility for control.
>
> To deal with these new problems will require a new conservation. We must not only protect the countryside and save it from destruction, we must restore what has been destroyed and salvage the beauty and charm of our cities. Our conservation must be not just the classic conservation of protection and development, but a creative conservation of restoration and innovation. Its concern is not with nature alone, but with the total relation between man and the world around him.[4]

The President called for a White House Conference on Natural Beauty to produce new ideas and approaches for enhancing the beauty of America. That conference was held in the spring of 1965, and has already resulted in plans for action. Among the more important measures recently passed by Congress, for example, are the Land and Water Conservation Fund Act and the establishment of the new Bureau of Outdoor Recreation, the Water Resources Research Act, the Wilderness Act, the act establishing the Public Land Law Review Commission and its companion measures, an urban improvement and beautification

4. The White House Message on Natural Beauty to the Congress of the United States, February 8, 1965 (mimeo release of the text of the message), p. 1.

program, the Water Resources Planning Act, the Clean Air Act, the Water Quality Act, the Highway Beautification Act. A number of new national parks and recreation areas have been established, and pending before Congress at the present time are various bills dealing with a National Wild Rivers Preservation System, greater controls on the use of pesticides and on air and water pollution, and a proposed new program of ecological research of the natural environmental systems in the United States. And these are only a few of the more significant subjects, all directly concerned with reversing the rapid deterioration in the quality of the environment.

How did this country get into such a predicament in the first place? One of the basic sources of difficulty has been the assumption underlying our economic system which equates the quality of life with the production of goods for private consumption. This made some sense in the past when the satisfaction of basic requirements absorbed the energies and incomes of most of our people. Under these conditions the annual increase in production—what economists call the Gross National Product—could be considered a chief measure of national vigor. But in the last few decades, the successes of the economic system have been phenomenal, and as the basic necessities of food, shelter, and clothing are met, the production of less vital commodities has expanded. As one noted economist, Kenneth Galbraith of Harvard, put it, there is diminishing emphasis on steel and bread grains in the economy and more on the production of electric golf carts and electric toothbrushes. "Questions may arise," he said, "whether national vigor is to be measured by ability to have dental hygiene without muscular effort or athletic endeavor while sitting down. Economic growth consists increasingly of items of luxury consumption. Thus, we perform the considerable feat of converting the enjoyment of luxury into an index of national virtues." [5]

It is not only highly dubious but embarrassing to continue

5. Kenneth Galbraith, "Economics v. the Quality of Life," *Encounter Magazine*, January 1965 (Vol. XXIV, No. 1), p. 32.

emphasizing the Gross National Product as the principal symbol of progress.

During the last ten years Resources for the Future, a subsidiary of the Ford Foundation, has engaged in a detailed statistical analysis of the prospects for natural resource commodities in the United States.[6] The outlook revealed by their economic studies is a highly optimistic one, disclosing that in spite of the enormously increased use of resource commodities over the past several decades, the real costs per unit of product have generally declined or remained constant. No major scarcity has developed in resources during the last sixty years or so, despite the fears of conservationists, and over the next generation—that is, up until the year 2000—this nation will not experience any significant long-term shortages of resource commodities that would have an adverse effect upon the economy. In substance, they found that despite our rapidly increasing population and per capita consumption of raw materials, the rapid rate of technological change in this country seems to be insuring that there will be no serious scarcity in the quantity of natural resource commodities required in the orderly growth of our economy.[7]

But while these economists are highly optimistic about the ability of this nation's natural resource base to meet quantitative demands for raw materials, they are much less certain about the future quality of the physical environment. They have concluded

6. Hans H. Landsberg, Leonard L. Fischman and Joseph L. Fisher, *Resources in America's Future: Patterns of Requirements and Availabilities, 1960–2000.* Baltimore: Johns Hopkins Press, 1963.

7. Scientific and technological advances have enormously increased agricultural production per acre; they have permitted the output of mineral commodities from low-grade ores at no increase in cost; they have opened up new sources of cheap energy, and produced a vast array of synthetic products that are being used as substitutes for scarcer and hence more expensive raw materials. The process of technological change has itself been institutionalized. Government, industry, academic institutions, and a variety of research entities with generous financial support are dedicated to scientific research, and the rate at which technological knowledge is being acquired is expected to accelerate at a rapid pace in the years ahead. With this momentum, it is difficult for these economists to believe that natural resource shortages in the traditional sense will plague the United States, at least within the foreseeable future.

in various subsequent publications that "a more productive world is not necessarily a better world;" [8] that "for the future, the quality of growth will be as much a part of the standard of living as the sheer amounts of things, and probably more so as people's appetite for material things become more nearly satiated;" [9] and in a very recent publication, itself entitled *Quality of the Environment,* it was concluded that "long before we are aware of an impending 'running out' [of natural resource products] we may come to be acutely aware of something else that is happening to us; a gradual growing stream of stimuli that produce an increasing dissatisfaction and, unfortunately, a dissatisfaction with which the individual finds it very hard to cope;" and finally that "many of our [economic] activities of production, movement and consumption do, unfortunately, inflict unwanted penalties on others . . . [and] in many cases, these unwanted effects are taken account of very inadequately or not at all by our politico-economic system." [10]

It is a refreshing sign to see that economists are finally becoming aware of these imperfections in the economic system. Economic theory and reasoning can continue to make a substantial contribution to the handling of difficult environmental problems, but this contribution will fall far short of its potential unless more economists succeed in escaping the dogma which requires them to view the economy as a delicate, self-regulating mechanism that has only to be left alone to produce the greatest satisfaction for all. What they have considered as minor market defects (that is, what the economist likes to call "external diseconomies") are, in fact, producing very serious side effects of

8. Harold J. Barnett and Chandler Morse, *Scarcity and Growth: The Economics of Natural Resource Availability* (Baltimore: The Johns Hopkins Press, 1963), p. 249 (see especially the last chapter on "National Resources and the Quality of Life," pp. 252–66).

9. Joseph L. Fisher, "Natural Resources and Economic Development" (speech by the President of Resources for the Future, Inc.), March 8, 1965 (mimeo), pp. 19–20.

10. Orris C. Herfindahl and Allen V. Kneese, *Quality of the Environment: An Economic Approach to Some Problems in Using Land, Water and Air* (Baltimore: The Johns Hopkins Press, 1965), p. v.

a qualitative nature, effects whose amelioration demands our best efforts. Technology has made it possible for the economy to grow rapidly without fear of resource scarcity, but it is a two-edged sword whose effects cannot entirely be controlled. As the English economist Joan Robinson has pleaded, surely values which can be measured in terms of money are not the only ones that ought to count.[11]

While our Malthusian fears may be eased somewhat by the new knowledge of the powers of technology, the same cannot be said about our prospects of maintaining the quality of the environment in the face of expected population increases. At the present rate of growth, America's population will double in less than fifty years, and such growth at the current high standard of living means that people inevitably destroy amenities for each other. A recent study by the Population Reference Bureau reports, for example, that it may soon become necessary to resort to rigid rationing of the use of the national parks, permitting each citizen a brief crowded holiday once every five years, then every ten, fifteen, or twenty years as population increases.[12] These data have been over-dramatized; nevertheless there is a close relationship between population growth and our ability—or inability—to solve a number of serious problems of environmental deterioration. Conflicts of value that cannot long continue to be ignored throng upon us.

Finally, there is what may be termed the administrative dilemma. This is related to but goes beyond the difficulty, mentioned in the previous chapter, of obtaining cooperation and coordination among competing bureaucracies. In the growth of the American political system separate agencies have been established to handle public responsibilities for a particular portion of the natural environment—either a given land area or a specific natural resource. Each has become highly professionalized with

11. For a critical analysis of this problem see Joan Robinson, *Economic Philosophy: An Essay on the Progress of Economic Thought* (New York: Doubleday & Company, 1964), p. 148 ff.

12. Population Reference Bureau release dated June 15, 1964.

respect to its particular function, and each has become surrounded by specialized pressure groups attempting to influence public policies to serve their particular needs and values; but no one in public life is charged with concern for the total environment as such. Each separate agency may be doing its job well, with coordination among the agencies at a high level. Yet each may be contributing unknowingly, unavoidably or unconcernedly to overall environmental deterioration. A public highway is planned in a manner that saves the taxpayer money but destroys scenic, recreational, or wildlife values. An agency sprays a forest with DDT to protect it from destructive pests without adequate knowledge of the impact on other living things. A superb park is established, but no one takes the responsibility to protect access routes from cluttered and unsightly commercial developments. A pulp mill is constructed in a national forest to use the timber on a sustained yield basis in keeping with a multiple land use plan, but the agency disclaims any responsibility for control of air and water pollution to protect other values. Such examples are plentiful. Some are acts of omission rather than commission. In some cases the objective was honorable, the destruction unintentional. In other cases the problem was not foreseen, or the responsibility was evaded, or there was no apparent legal jurisdiction to act. Regardless of the causes, the effects are the same; and in this age of rapid man-made change, even slight mistakes or oversights can have a cumulative effect of disastrous proportions on the environment.

The problem stems in part from the antiquated governmental machinery for decision-making, but it is also a product of the education of public officials in the resources fields. The trend is toward greater and greater specialization at a time when the growing conflicts among land and resources uses demand a broader and more comprehensive knowledge of intricate ecological interrelationships in the natural and human environments. Lynton K. Caldwell, a political scientist who has undertaken an intensive study of this problem, recently summarized the problem:

> If government has no general mandate for safeguarding the total environment, its policies will be directed toward only those parts of it that have been identified for political action. . . . In the absence of an ecological perception of the environment in its interrelated totality, neither electorates nor party leaders nor public administrators give serious attention to the overall effect of government action on environmental change.
>
> In the search for a sounder basis for public environmental policy, we are ultimately forced back upon the basis of all political action—popular perceptions of needs and values. . . . The search for sounder environmental decisions thus leads to a concentrated educational effort that will open people's minds to comprehension of the universality of nature and of man's relation to the natural world as revealed by science and increasingly influenced by political action.[13]

Attempts are being made to overcome some of these perplexing difficulties by developing new tools and approaches for public decision-making, but as Caldwell points out, those so far developed leave much to be desired. One concept, that of multiple use, has seemed a logical avenue toward determining how best to serve varied interests in an environment. But it is difficult to determine priorities among conflicting uses and values, and one is hard put to it to make discriminating choices. Another concept, that of weighing environment-affecting decisions on the basis of costs and benefits, is limited at the outset to circumstances in which measurement can be expressed in monetary or other tangible terms. Some day a comprehensive environmental administration must become a reality for, as Caldwell concludes, it does not follow that if the lesser jobs are pursued with diligence, the greater ones will take care of themselves.[14]

These economic, demographic, and political problems are grave ones, but the situation is not hopeless, for there are signs that qualitative values will be given more concerted attention by scientists, scholars, politicians, and administrators in the years immediately ahead. Public apathy is beginning to give way; this could portend a revolutionary effort of commitment and invest-

13. Lynton K. Caldwell, "Public Policies and Environmental Values," *I.U.C.N. Bulletin*, April–June 1964, p. 2.

14. Lynton K. Caldwell, "Environment: A New Focus for Public Policy?" *Public Administration Review*. September 1963 (Vol. XXIII, No. 3), pp. 132–39.

ment to achieve quality of life out of the quantity of prosperity.

To many Alaskans this growing national emphasis on the maintenance of the total environment does not seem applicable to their state which is so fortunately blessed with natural scenic beauty, wildlife resources, open spaces, wilderness, and other lands that have hardly been touched by man. The editor of the largest newspaper in Alaska made this point when he said:

> Alaska is more than 99 percent wilderness. The threat of dissipating such a vast area by economic development must be several generations away. Shouldn't economic development be allowed to take place with as few restrictions as possible, at least temporarily. . . . Why not provide the needed protection in the other states, and let this state remain in status quo at least until development has penetrated a bit further into the vast wilderness? [15]

The fallacy of this logic is that it casts the issue in such a way as to present only two possible alternatives: either we allow economic development with no controls, or we remain 99 percent wilderness. This is the familiar pose of the ostrich. Once again, we are faced with that kind of dichotomous thinking which has led many Alaskans to pose the basic problem in the form: either development or conservation.

There is no denying Alaska's need for sound economic development. The point has been emphasized throughout this study. By the same token, despite the relatively slow rate of growth that has occurred so far, one does not have to look far to find evidence of man-made environmental deterioration following in its wake. The highway approaches to Alaska's few major cities are for the most part as sadly blighted as any to be found elsewhere. Once inviting countrysides surrounding the cities are being obliterated in a frenzy of helter-skelter commercial and housing developments, with garbage dumps and junk yards and the unreplanted gravel pits freely visible. Rural slums consisting of rows of dilapidated shacks on small lots radiate out from the towns—a product of misguided federal land laws that require the construction of a

15. "Man-Made Deep Freeze Could Throttle Alaska," editorial in *Anchorage Daily Times,* July 31, 1962.

"minimum structure" to gain title to "free" land. Interspersed here and there are the stump farms of the unsuccessful homesteaders or other settlers who ran out of money and quit, leaving downed timber and stumps as a memento. There are the scars on the landscape made by the great gold dredges—acre after acre of upturned land that no longer can sustain life—and the eroded wasteland left by the hydraulic miners.

There are the many scars left by the federal government itself —land for an antenna or some other government facility cleared by pushing trees and underbrush into great piles and leaving them to rot; the stacks and stacks of rusty, worthless oil drums that have been allowed to accumulate year after year around many government posts; the abandoned government installations where no effort has been made to prevent deterioration or to return the land to its original status. And there are the criss-cross scars stretching out across the muskeg and up over the alpine tundra made by the specially designed tracked vehicles of the hunters, nearly all of whom consider themselves ardent conservationists; scars that may take a century or more to heal because of the delicate and fragile ecological balance in this northern subarctic environment. Many more miles of these vehicle trails have been made by miners and seismic exploration crews of private firms and government agencies.

Admittedly, this environmental deterioration has not progressed to the stage it has in many parts of the country which now require massive, costly long-term programs to rebuild and repair the mistakes of the past. It is for precisely this reason that the challenge of Alaska's future is so exciting. The concept of the total environment as a possible focus for public policy is only now beginning to crystallize, but it seems to offer the chance for a synthesis of the goals of the "either-or" thinkers; to point the way toward development decisions that place the quality of the environment on a par with the quantity of resources produced. In pioneering this new approach to development, Alaska could evolve a new and better way of life in harmony with both the land and the deeper realities of life, a way that could be a significant contribution to its own future and the nation rather than a mindless echo of what has gone before.

In years past, Alaska was thought of primarily as a place to go to work, to acquire money, and to leave. The population was highly transient. In the last decade, however, more and more people are coming to Alaska with an altogether different purpose in mind. They have become dissatisfied with their hurly-burly, complex, and often meaningless existence that offers comfort, entertainment and security but little real satisfaction. They are well enough off financially; but happiness seems to be absent from their lives, and they come to Alaska seeking a new environment that will fulfill this need. A surprising number set out immediately to try to recreate exactly what they left behind, never recognizing that in the process they may be destroying what it was that brought them here. But a large proportion of those who come and stay to make Alaska their permanent home are held by more basic values. Governor William A. Egan expressed this well in a speech entitled, "What the Future Holds for Alaska." Said the governor:

> Those of us who live in Alaska enjoy and cherish those things that brought and keep us here: the mountains, the sea, the lakes and rivers, the forests, the elbow room, and the sense of purpose that comes from building—with the land and its elements—the good rich life that is possible in mid-twentieth century America.[16]

It would be folly if public policies were not carefully designed with the needs and desires of this vital, growing segment of the population constantly in mind.

A current piece of Alaska tourist promotion concludes with the "hurry-hurry" tone of a sideshow barker: "Remember, too, that much you will see and enjoy—today, will, with the onrush of 'civilization' be gone forever—tomorrow."[17] This outcome is possible but by no means inevitable, for there is growing proof

16. Second Inaugural Address, January 1963.

17. Advertisement in *The Milepost, Travel Guide to the Land of the Midnight Sun,* reported in George W. Rogers, *The Future of Alaska* (Baltimore: Johns Hopkins Press), 1962, p. 52.

that industrial progress and natural beauty can exist side by side. What happens in Alaska could prove to be a kind of reformation; a discarding of the old mythology and a creative adventure in shaping new approaches to land and resource policy adjusted both to nature and to man's needs and values in the modern world. It is an opportunity that is extremely rare, for this fresh northern environment is opening up for development at a time when a new and more profound concept of conservation is being formulated and pressed vigorously on the national level—a concept that relates every living thing on this planet to the total environment. Much depends on the direction in which the American personality is developing; for in this age of science and technology, man's environment is a reflection of self.

REFERENCE MATTER

The Maps

This series of maps has been arranged for easy comparison of physical, economic, and social features of the Alaska landscape. By comparing the various resource maps with the map showing lands in federal reserves, it is possible to see in a very general way which lands with known resource values will likely be considered for selection by the state in the years ahead. The map showing the Indian lands claimed by the various Eskimo, Indian, and Aleut groups makes it very clear however that many of the lands the state might wish to select are also claimed by these native groups. This and other conflicts of land use are certain to intensify as the state moves further into the hinterlands with its land selection program.

Information for Maps 5, 6, 7, 10, 11, and 12 was supplied by the Bureau of Land Management.

All maps in this section courtesy of the University of Wisconsin Cartographic Laboratory

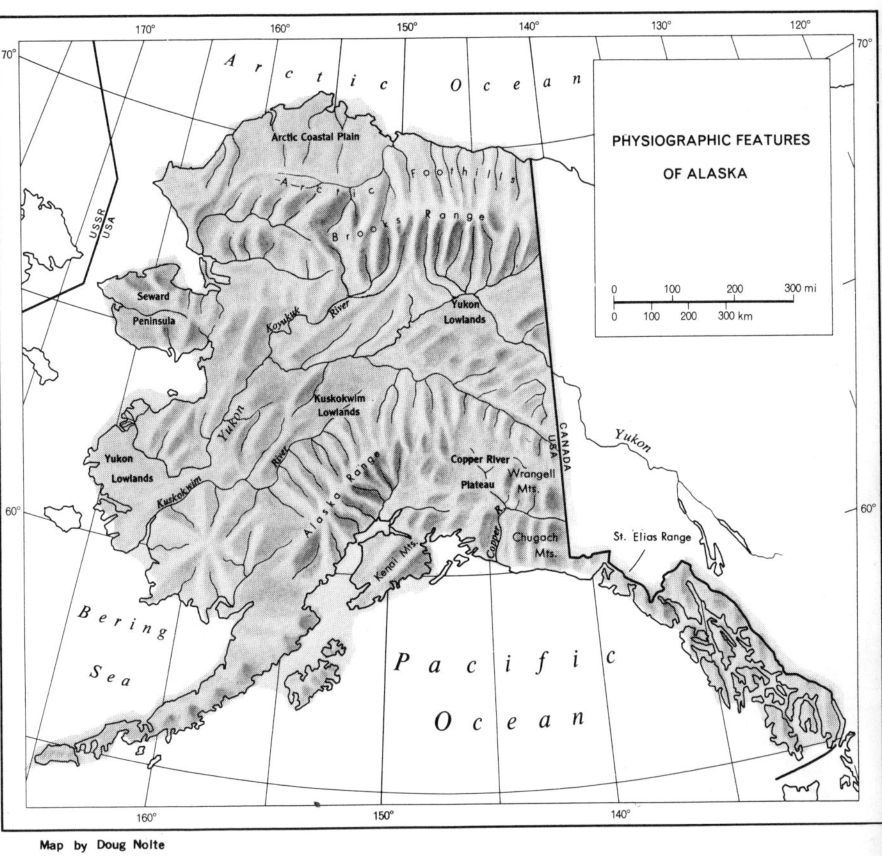

Map by Doug Nolte

Map 1. Physiographic Provinces of Alaska

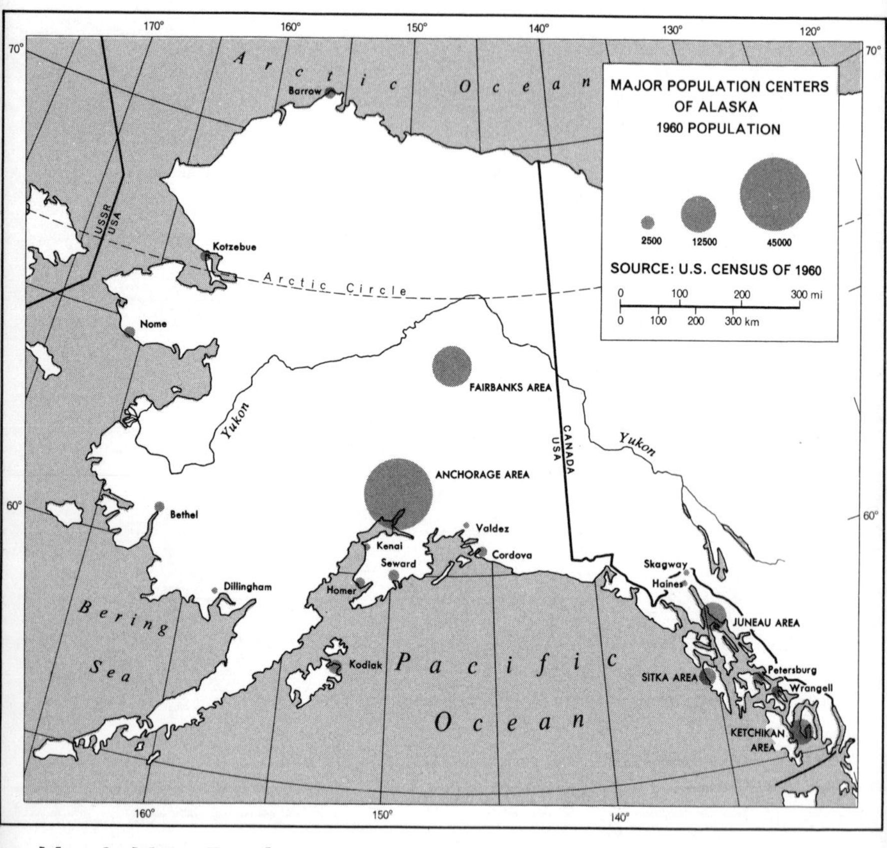

Map 2. Major Population Centers of Alaska, 1960 Population

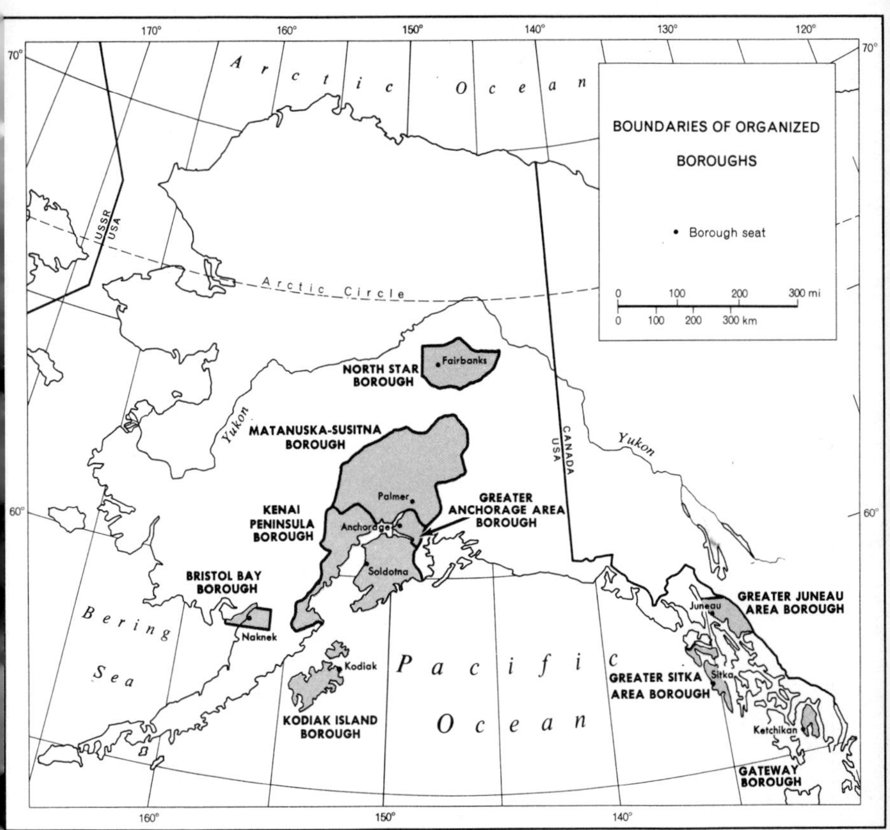

Map 3. Boundaries of Organized Boroughs in Alaska, 1965

Borough	Population (1960 Census)	Size (sq. miles)
Bristol Bay	1,015	1,200
Gateway	8,874	1,250
Greater Anchorage	66,559 est.*	1,500
Greater Juneau	9,745	3,100
Greater Sitka	6,690	2,900
Kenai Peninsula	9,053	15,000
Kodiak Island	4,438†	4,500
Matanuska-Susitna	5,188	23,000
North Star	25,000‡	7,500

* Excluding residents of Elmendorf AFB and Fort Richardson
† Excluding residents of the Kodiak Naval Station
‡ Excluding residents of Eielson AFB and Fort Wainwright

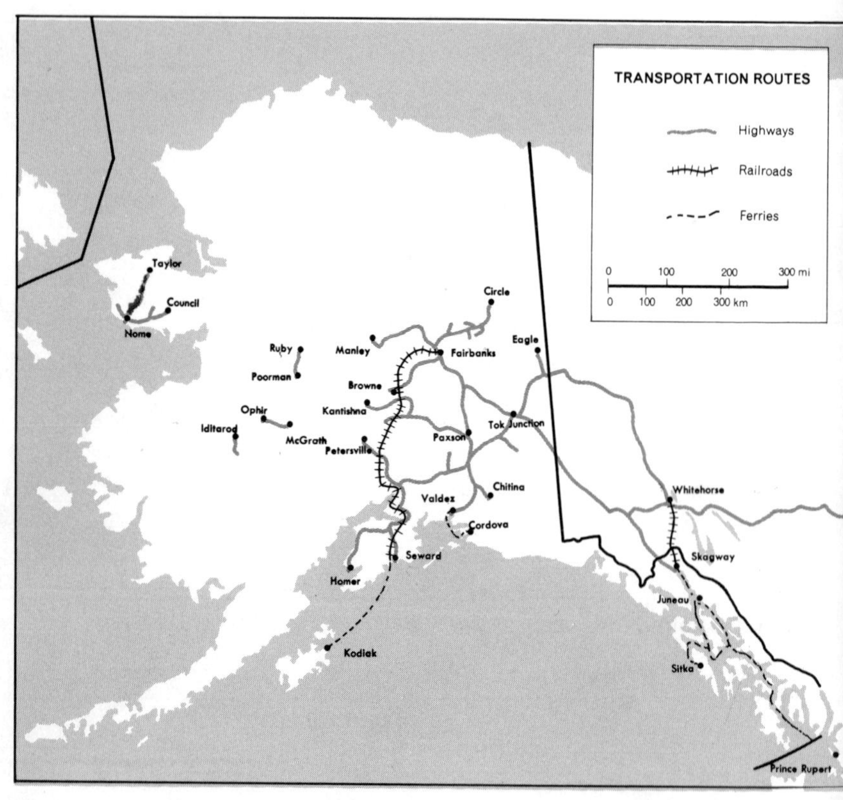

Map 4. Transportation Routes in Alaska, 1965

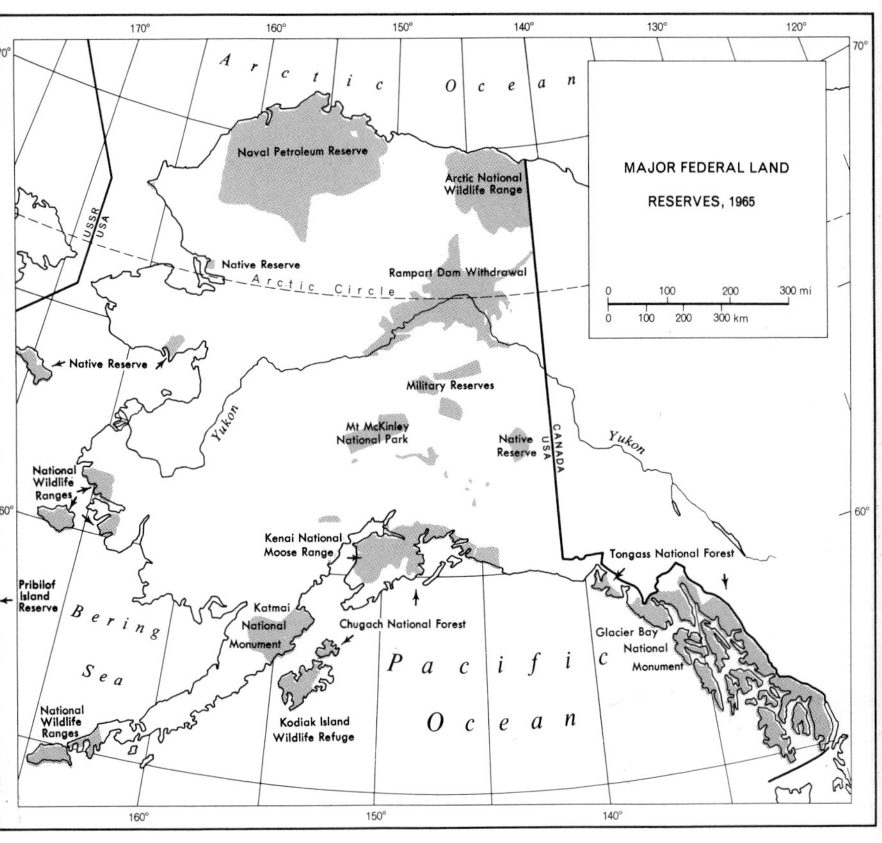

Map 5. Major Federal Land Reserves, Through 1965

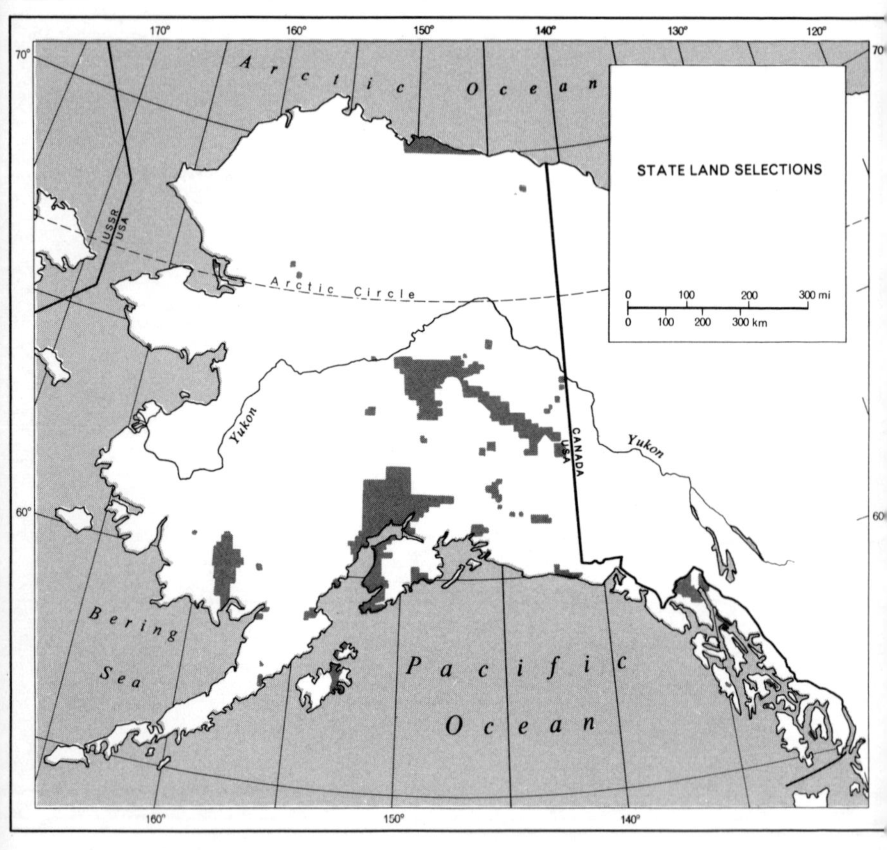

Map 6. State Land Selections, Through 1965

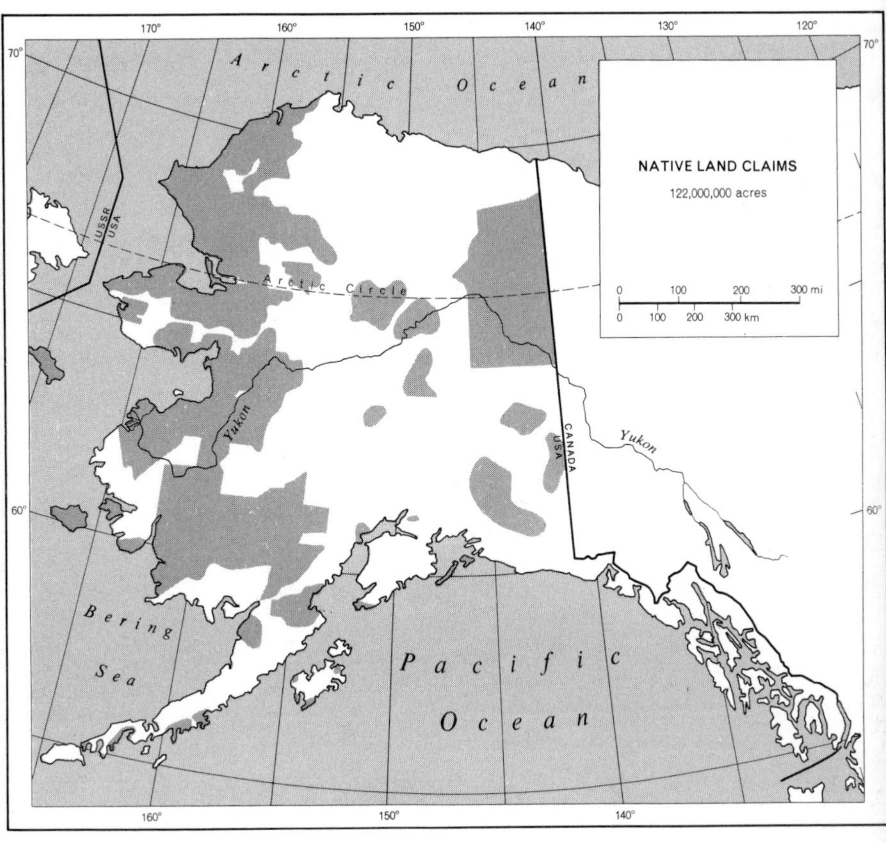

Map 7. Native Land Claims in Alaska, Based on Aboriginal Rights of Eskimo, Indian, and Aleut Groups

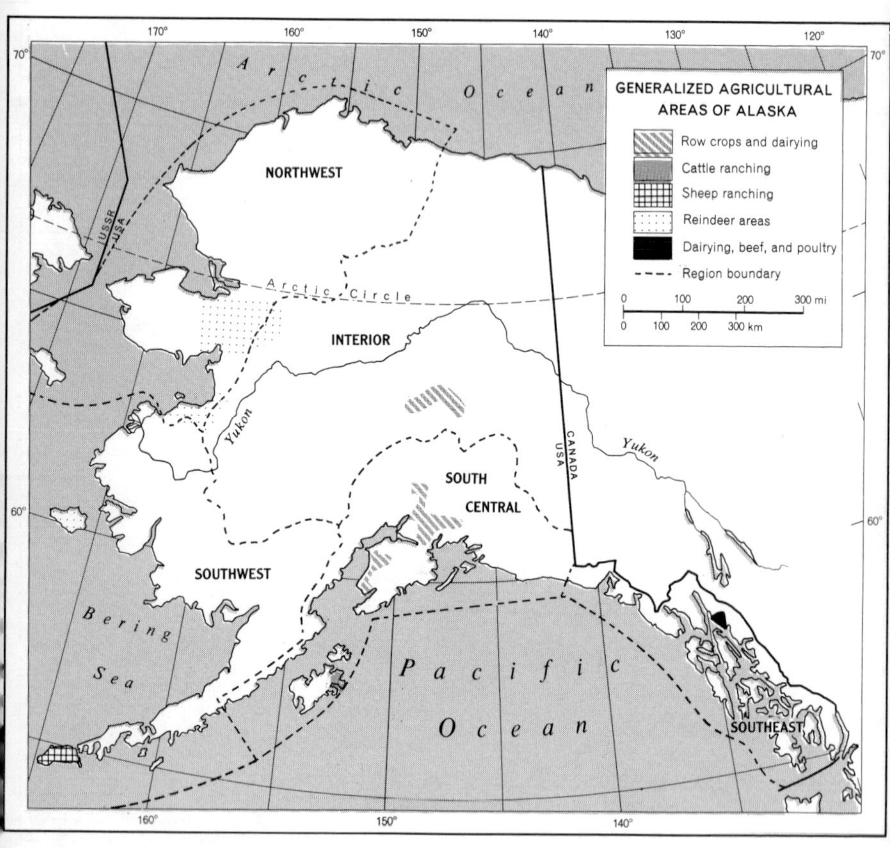

Map 8. Generalized Agricultural Areas of Alaska, 1965

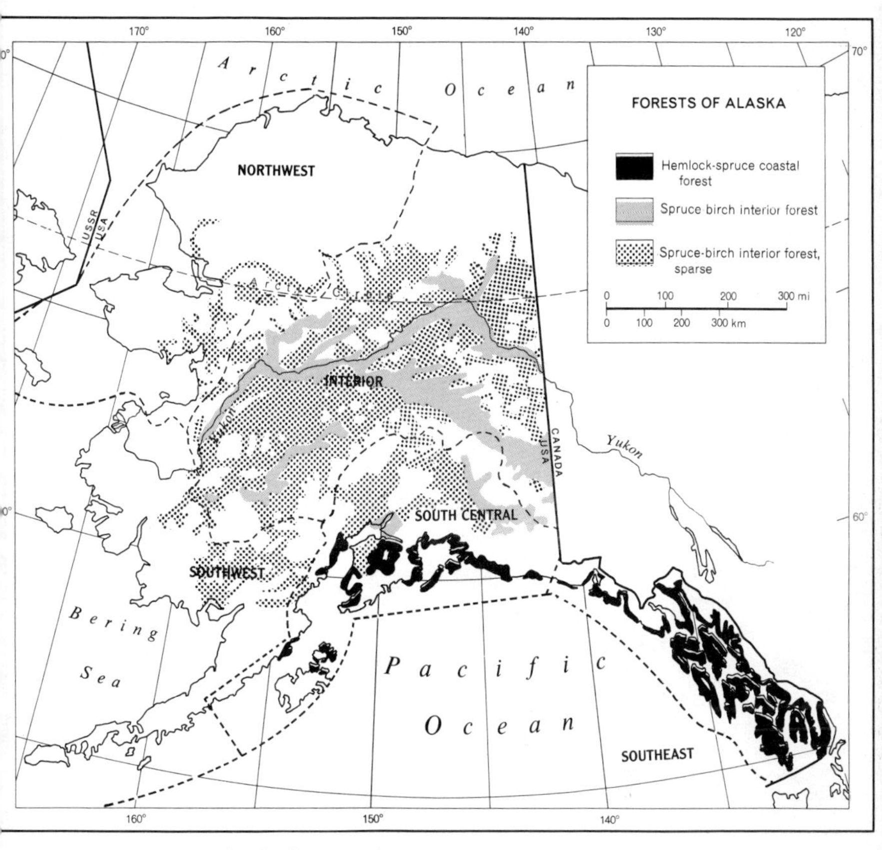

Map 9. Forests of Alaska, 1965

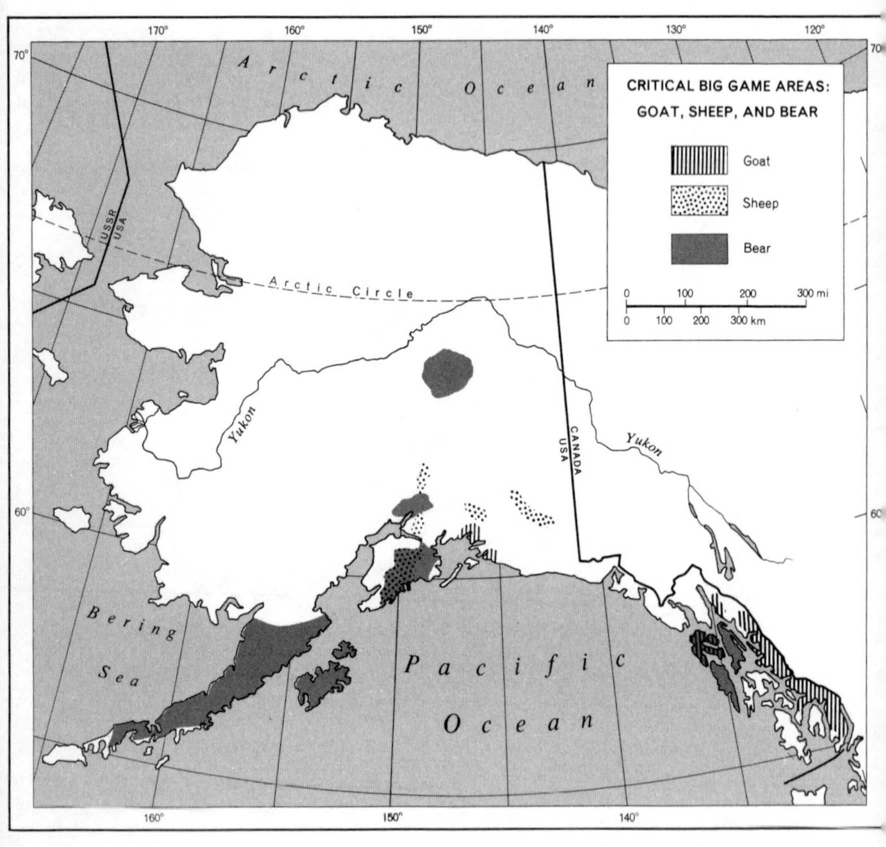

Map 10. Critical Big Game Areas, 1965: Goat, Sheep, and Bear

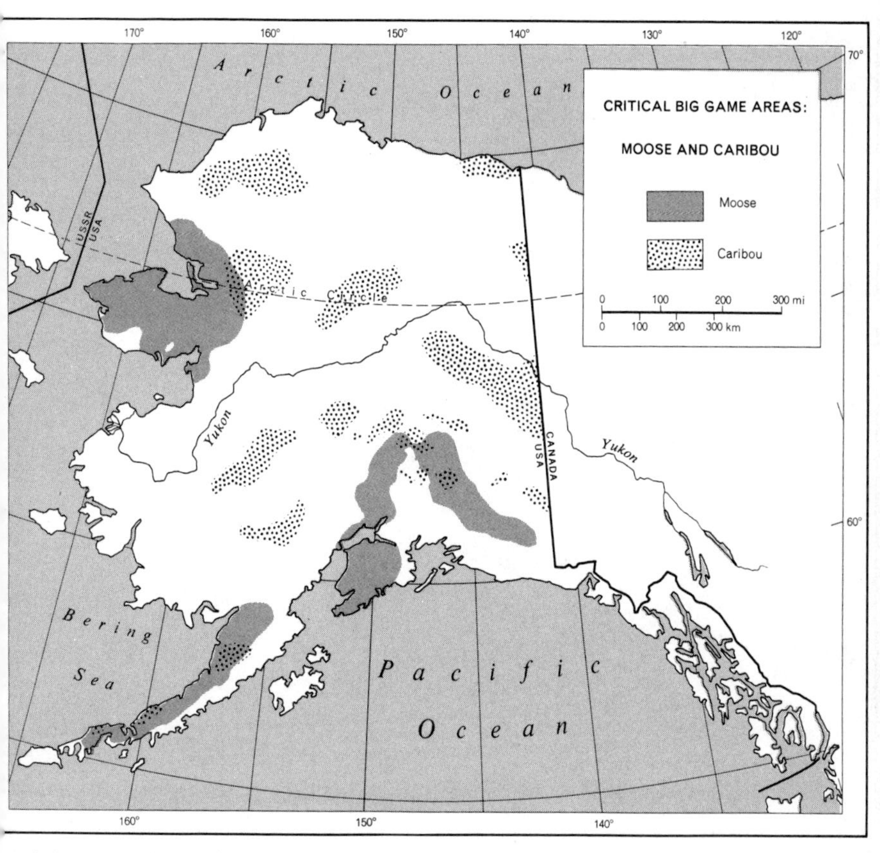

Map 11. Critical Big Game Areas, 1965: Moose and Caribou

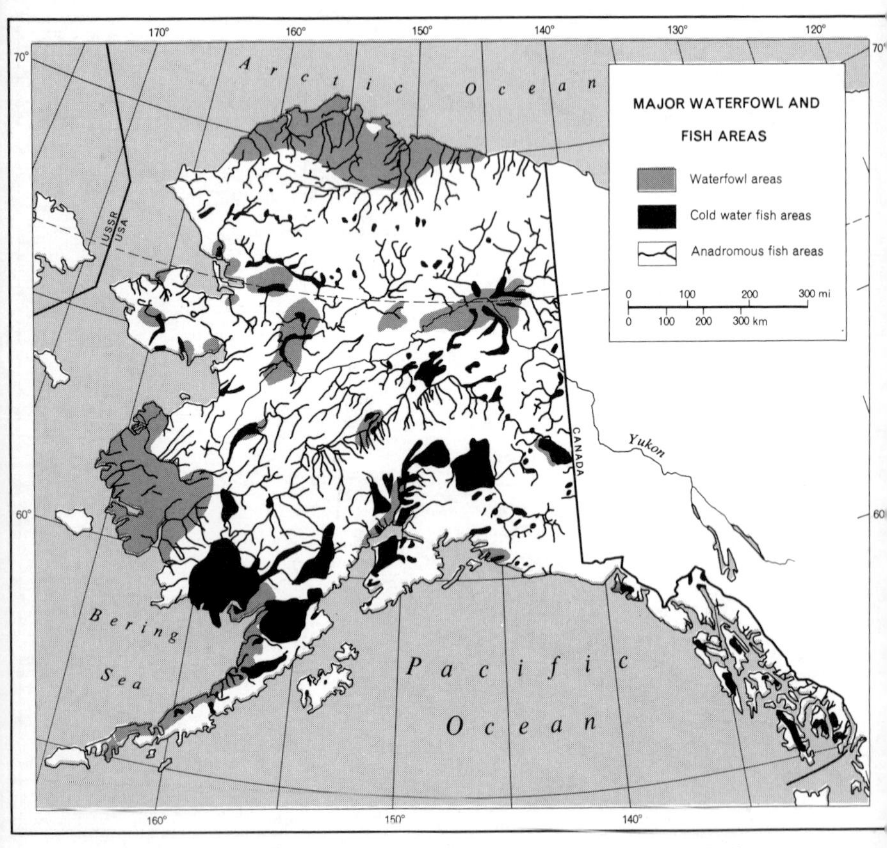

Map 12. Major Waterfowl and Fish Areas in Alaska, 1965

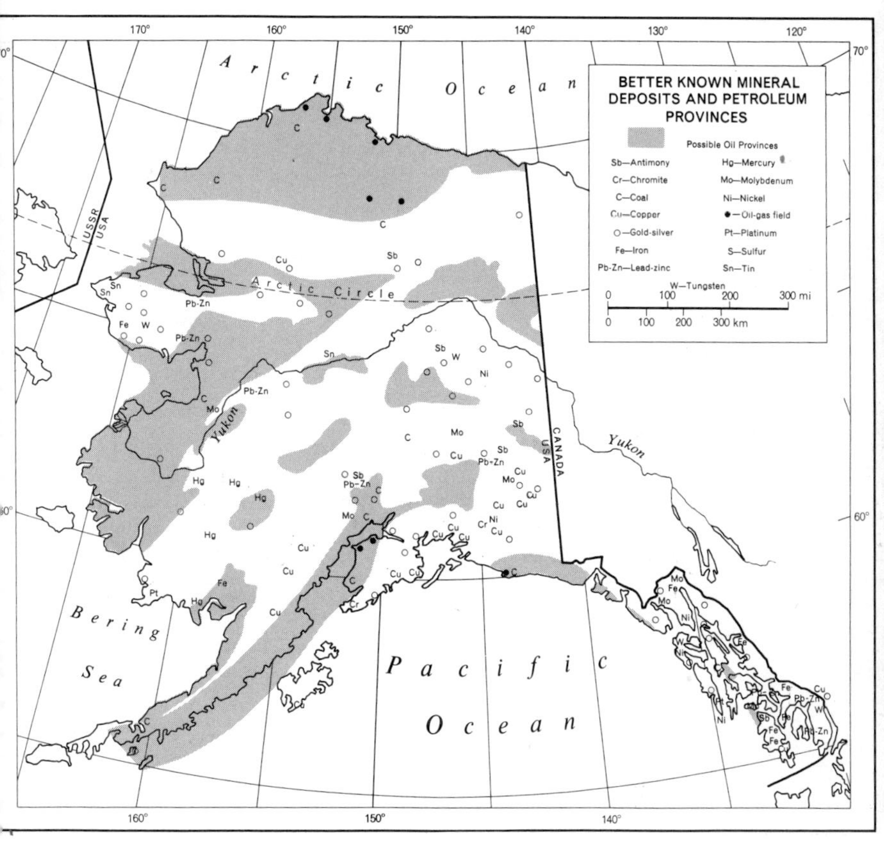

Map 13. Better Known Mineral Deposits and Petroleum Provinces, 1965

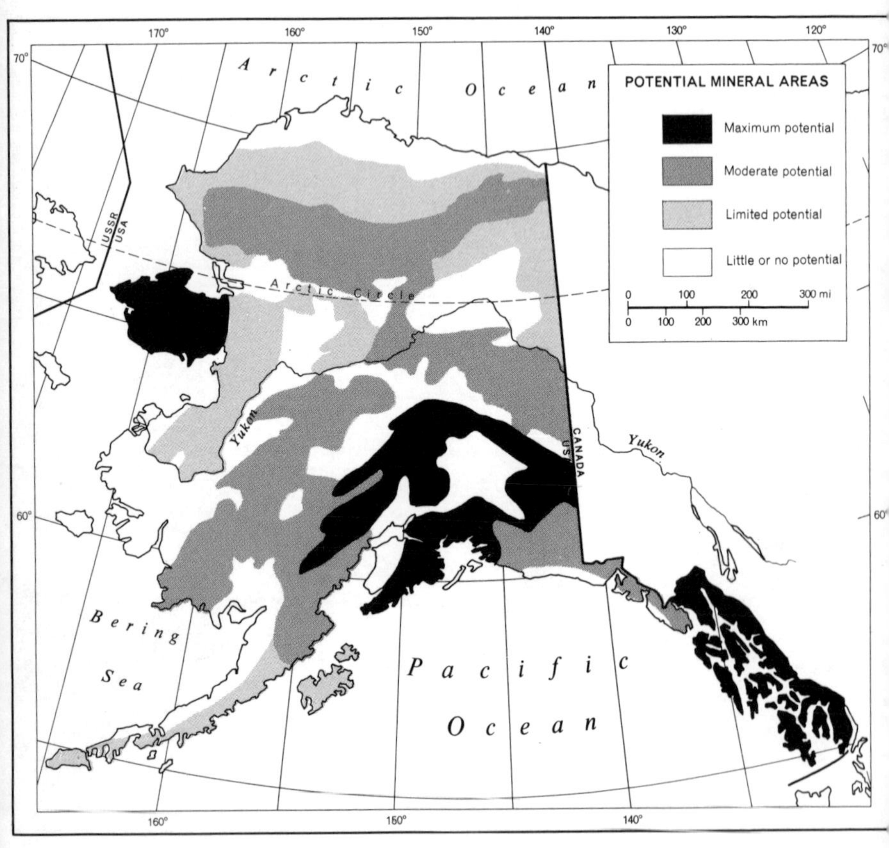

Map 14. Potential Mineral Areas of Alaska, 1965

TABLE A

Revenue from State Lands

Fiscal Year 1959 to 1964 with Estimates to 1970

Fiscal Year (as of June 30)	Land Lease Rentals	Land Sales	Resource Sales	Mineral Lease Bonuses	Mineral Lease Rentals	Mineral Production Royalties	Total
1959					$ 10		$ 10
1960	$ 1,047	$ 150	$ 20,797	$ 4,021,031	90,312		4,133,337
1961	118	4,000	22,126	1,551,686	159,968		1,737,898
1962	10,671	62,849	8,289	20,298,289	954,203		21,334,301
1963	13,687	87,749	40,844	17,863,866	1,050,151	$ 27,510	19,083,807
1964	20,388	257,795	46,684	4,738,348	1,181,172	36,440	6,280,827
				Estimated			
1965	$28,000	$315,000	$ 70,500	$ 5,614,000	$2,042,000	$ 100,000	$ 8,169,500
1966	31,000	320,000	74,500	2,500,000	2,527,500	559,000	6,012,000
1967	33,000	325,000	86,000	1,530,000	3,059,000	1,359,100	6,392,100
1968	34,500	330,000	102,000	1,116,000	3,328,000	2,096,400	7,006,900
1969	36,000	335,000	133,500	925,000	3,582,500	2,502,600	7,514,600
1970	36,500	340,000	149,300	725,000	3,660,500	2,829,500	7,740,800

Revenue from University lands and school lands is excluded.

Source of data: State of Alaska, Department of Administration.

TABLE B

Total State Revenues from State and Federal Lands and Resources as Percent of the Total State General Fund, Fiscal Years 1959 to 1964 with Estimates to 1970

Fiscal Year	Total State Revenues from State and Federal Lands and from Resources	As Percent of Total State General Fund
1959	$ 3,286,439	12.4
1960	10,897,048	22.7
1961	5,452,268	13.5
1962	26,675,116	38.9
1963	28,554,582	39.9
1964	15,750,416	23.7
Total	$90,615,869	28.2
	Estimated	
1965	$18,995,500	24.5
1966	16,815,000	24.2
1967	17,865,800	26.8
1968	18,339,300	29.9
1969	18,463,200	26.2
1970	18,309,400	25.4

Excluded are fish and game, and income from school lands and University lands accruing to special funds.

Source of data: State of Alaska, Department of Administration.

TABLE C

Total Operating Costs of the Division of Lands Compared with Total Income from State Lands Calendar Years 1959–64

Calendar Year	Total Operating Costs	Ratio of Income to Costs
1959–61	$1,221,278	13.9 to 1
1962	883,279	33.2 to 1
1963	1,151,667	5.7 to 1
1964	1,137,631	5.5 to 1
Average 1959–64	732,309	13.5 to 1

Source of data: State of Alaska, Department of Natural Resources, Division of Lands.

TABLE D

Total Net Operating Costs of the Division of Lands Compared with Total Recurrent Income from State Lands Calendar Years 1959–64

Calendar Year	Net Operating Costs	Ratio of Recurrent Income to Net Costs
1959–61	$1,185,278	1.1 to 1
1963	819,574	2.1 to 1
1963	987,365	1.9 to 1
1964	962,631	2.1 to 1
Average 1959–64	659,141	1.8 to 1

Source of data: State of Alaska, Department of Natural Resources, Division of Lands.

TABLE E

Recurrent and Non-recurrent Revenues from State Lands
Calendar Years 1959–64

	1959–64	1962	1963	1964	Cumulative Total
Total revenues received	$16,930,139	$29,345,768	$6,591,013	$10,362,603 *	$63,229,523 *
Bonuses and surplus property	15,577,000	27,608,727	4,763,488	8,309,858 *	56,259,073 *
Recurrent type	$ 1,353,139	$ 1,737,041	$1,827,525	$2,052,745	$ 6,970,450

* Includes balance payable in competitive oil and gas lease sale of Dec. 9, 1964, amounting to $4.1 million.

Source: State of Alaska, Department of Natural Resources, Division of Lands, *Annual Report*, 1964.

TABLE F

Revenues from State Lands by Type of Grants and Resources
Calendar Years 1959–64

Receipts by Grants	School	University	Mental Health	General	Total
1959–61	$ 390,295	$ 645,937	$ 7,130,741	$ 8,450,269	$16,617,242
1962	257,854	255,640	91,596	28,422,113	29,027,203
1963	367,438	224,930	2,931,158	2,928,449	6,451,975
1964	308,509	25,329	697,371	5,170,425 *	6,201,634 *
Cumulative Total	$1,324,096	$ 1,151,836	$10,850,866	$44,971,256 *	$58,298,054
				Fees	831,469
				Total	$59,129,523 *

Receipts by Resources	Lands	Minerals	Forestry	Fees	Total
1959–61	$1,059,997	$15,549,756	$ 7,489	$ 312,897	$16,930,139
1962	352,113	28,658,442	16,648	318,565	29,345,768
1963	597,595	5,817,712	36,668	139,038	6,591,013
1964	601,826	5,536,703 *	63,105	60,969	6,262,603 *
Cumulative Total	$2,611,531	$55,562,613 *	$ 123,910	$ 831,469	$59,129,523 *

* Competitive sale of Dec. 9, 1964, brought in high bids totaling $5,611,749.97. Only 20 percent down payment required. Dec. 12, 1964, balance due, $4.1 million, not included in above totals.

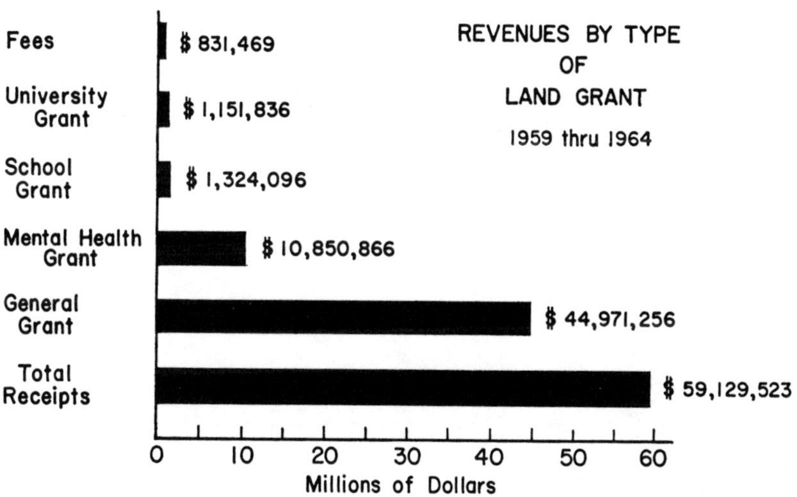

Source: State of Alaska, Department of Natural Resources, Division of Lands, *Annual Report,* 1964.

State Land Selection Progress by Type of Grant in Acres
Calendar Years 1959–64

Calendar Year		General	Mental Health	Community Grant: Public Domain	Community Grant: National Forest	School Lands ‡	University: University †	University: Tanana Valley ‡	Total
1959	Selected	1,094,864	312,385						1,407,249
	Tentatively approved *								
	Patented	144							144
1960	Selected	4,724,293	203,131	25,503			99,015		5,051,942
	Tentatively approved *	658,528	7,516						666,044
	Patented	55,900	973	1,085			46,526		104,484
1961	Selected	4,354,809	60,077	11,983					4,426,869
	Tentatively approved *	1,066,825	224,819						1,291,644
	Patented	123,580	34,844	44			31,925		190,393
1962	Selected	1,643,869	26,485		1,026				1,671,380
	Tentatively approved *	1,442,217	88,567	679			3,510		1,534,973
	Patented	341,810	84,312	53			10,510		436,685
1963	Selected	653,227	212,268	25			8		865,528
	Tentatively approved *	4,328,185	251,332				203		4,579,720
	Patented	173,527	94,023	582		3,091	9,254	585	281,062
1964	Selected	1,996,768	69,216	3,382	15,123	1,640	871		2,087,000
	Tentatively approved *	2,809,992	89,131	9,274					2,908,397
	Patented	223,279	131,032	2,996		3,942	815	1,108	363,172
Cumulative total									
	Selected	14,467,830	883,562	40,893	16,149	107,236 §	99,894	11,044 §	15,626,608 §
	Tentatively approved *	10,305,747	661,365	9,997			3,713		10,980,822
	Patented	918,240	345,184	4,760		97,298 §	99,030	7,387 §	1,471,899 §

* Acreage tentatively approved during year and under tentative approval at end of year; does not include lands on which tentative approval was received during year but which were subsequently patented.

† University lands became the responsibility of the Division after June 1960.

‡ The "in-place" grants to the schools (surveyed sections 16 & 36) and to the University (surveyed sections 33 in the Tanana Valley) were originally reported together, with separate figures given for the first time in 1963.

§ Totals include school lands selected and patented prior to the granting of statehood.

TABLE H

Annual Income from Upland Leases and Sales
Calendar Years 1961–64

	1961	1962	1963	1964
Lease income	$126,700	$135,192	$175,858 *	$192,730
Sale income	83,502	151,626	275,641	375,702
Material income	18,381	63,340	27,949	22,024
Misc. income	4,648	7,810	9,237	2,136
Total annual income	$233,231	$357,968	$488,685	$592,592

* Not including $100,552 in nonrecurring right-of-way income.

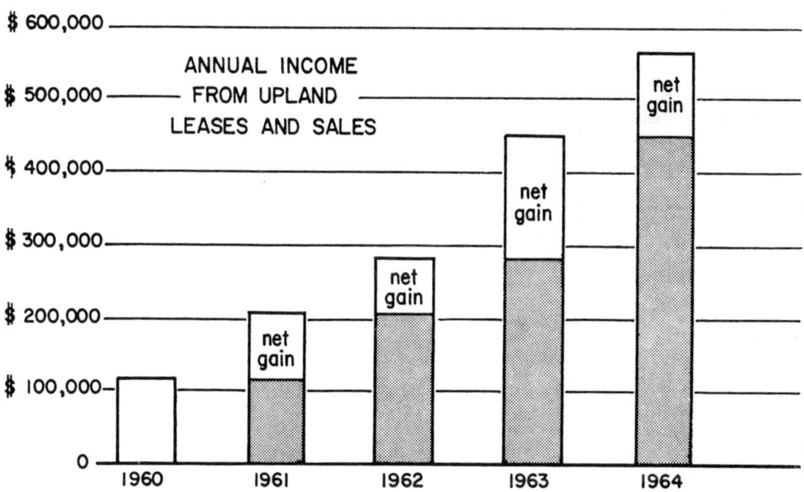

Source: State of Alaska, Department of Natural Resources, Division of Lands, *Annual Report*, 1964.

TABLE I

Competitive Oil and Gas Leasing of State Lands
Calendar Years 1959–64

	No. of Sales	Tracts Offered	Tracts Leased	Acres Leased	Bonus Bid
1959	1	37	32	77,831.00	$ 4,021,031.43
1960	2	53	35	39,372.27	442,979.85
1961	4	181	161	296,640.44	22,415,940.16
1962	2	97	84	265,498.33	15,719,233.60
1963	3 *	508	365 †	388,521.79 †	7,178,905.66 †
1964	1	610	347	739,663.00	5,611,749.97
Total	13	1,486	1,024	1,807,526.83	$55,389,840.67

Since 1959 a total of 399 leases have terminated, releasing 877,-396.90 acres. There are 625 competitive leases active, covering 930,-129.93 acres.

Table includes the results of the 13th sale held December 9, 1964, anticipating issuance of all leases.

* Sale #11 cancelled.

† Adjustment for 1963: 7 tracts not leased in #12 reduced acreage by 9,353.00 and the bonus by $12,484.53.

Source: State of Alaska, Department of Natural Resources, Division of Lands, *Annual Report*, 1964.

TABLE J

Noncompetitive Oil and Gas Leasing of State Lands
Calendar Years 1959–64

	1959–62 *	1963 *	1964 *	Total
State Offerings				
Tracts leased	211	83	107	483
Acres leased	488,327.02	176,697.21	116,970.28	979,208.51
Federal Transfers and Offers				
Leases transferred	68	58	14	279
Acres leased	56,612.32	86,127.95	6,413.95	236,229.18
Offers received	13	13	6	327
Offers recognized	3	14	4	25
Acreage	801.13	6,713.22	4,990.00	16,185.28
Terminations				
Leases terminated	23	114	138	281
Acres terminated	47,105.52	208,375.32	213,328.00	472,749.19
Total active leases	478	519	561	
Active acreage	782,664.49	843.827.55	758.873.78	
Annual rental	$391,322.25	$413,404.41	$373,340.25 †	

* Annual totals do not include leases issued but cancelled during the year.

† Includes some transferred federal leases at an annual rental of $0.25 per acre.

Source: State of Alaska, Department of Natural Resources, Division of Lands, *Annual Report,* 1964.

TABLE K

Federal Revenue Payments to the State of Alaska for Oil, Gas, and Coal Leasing on Federal Lands Calendar Years 1959–64

	Oil and Gas Rental	Oil and Gas Royalty	Coal Rental and Royalty	Total Payment Received
1959	$ 4,260.322 *	$ 12,678	$ 60,000 *	$ 4,333,000
1960	2,626.829 *	97,171	63,000 *	2,787,000
1961	1,828,868 *	1,640,132	86,000 *	3,555,000
1962	4,646,316 *	2,499,026	60,000 *	7,205,342
1963	4,491,987	3,859,989	94,153	8,446,129
1964	5,529,110	3,374,603	88,680	8,992,394
Total	$23,383,432	$11,483,599	$451,834	$35,318,865

* Estimated.

Source: State of Alaska, Department of Natural Resources, Division of Lands, *Annual Report,* 1964.

TABLE L

Timber Sales and Harvests from State Lands Calendar Years 1959–64

	Annual Sales		Annual Cut	
Year	Volume (MBF)	Value	Volume (MBF)	Value
1959	363	$ 575	—	—
1960	1,760	3,787	210	$ 629
1961	25,592	80,564	1,987	5,769
1962	14,755	34,211	6,872	19,990
1963	17,590	43,551	10,633	22,107
1964	37,644	109,180	18,144	59,151

Source: State of Alaska, Department of Natural Resources, Division of Lands, *Annual Report,* 1964.

Bibliography

Alaska Constitutional Convention. Report of the Committee on Resources (Committee Proposal No. 8). Fairbanks, December 1955. (Mimeographed)

American Association for the Advancement of Science. *Land and Water Use*. A symposium presented at the Denver meeting, December 27–29, 1961. Edited by Wynne Thorpe. Baltimore: The Horn Shafer Company, 1963.

Ashby, Andrew W. *Public Lands*. A land tenure study by the Food and Agriculture Organization of the United Nations, Rome, Italy, March 1956.

Bell, Roscoe, E. "Alaska—In the Wake of the Quake." Speech presented by Director of Alaska Division of Lands before City Club of Portland, Oregon, July 3, 1964. (Mimeographed)

———. "How to Acquire Government Land in Alaska." Reprint from *Alaska Sportsman Magazine*, Juneau, Alaska. (No date.)

———. "Land Policy Considerations in Management of State Lands." *Science in Alaska 1963*. Proceedings of the Fourteenth Alaskan Science Conference, Anchorage, Alaska, August 27–30, 1963. Alaska Division A.A.A.S., 1964.

———. "Your Land and My Land." Speech prepared by Director, Alaska Division of Lands, October 1, 1959. (Mimeographed)

Bowman, Wallace D. *Alaska's Outdoor Recreation Potential*. A Report to the Outdoor Recreation Resources Review Commission by the Conservation Foundation (ORRRC Study Report 9). Washington: Govt. Printing Office, 1962.

Carstensen, Vernon, ed. *The Public Lands: Studies in the History of the Public Domain*. Madison: The University of Wisconsin Press, 1963.

Clawson, Marion, R., Burnell Held and Charles H. Stoddard. *Land for the Future*. Published for Resources for the Future. Baltimore: The Johns Hopkins Press, 1960.

Dana, Samuel Trask, and Myron Krueger. *California Lands Ownership, Use, and Management*. The American Forestry Association. Narberth: Livingston Publishing Company, 1958.

———, John H. Allison and Russell N. Cunningham. *Minnesota Lands: Ownership, Use, and Management of Forest and Related Lands*.

Prepared for the American Forestry Association. Narberth: The Livingston Publishing Company, 1960.

DeLeonardis, Salvatore, and Herbert C. Lang. "Planning for Alaska's Future," *A Place to Live* (Yearbook of the U.S. Department of Agriculture, 1963). Washington: Govt. Printing Office, 1963.

Federal Reconstruction and Development Planning Commission for Alaska. *Response to Disaster*. Washington: Govt. Printing Office, September 1964.

Haig-Brown, Roderick. *The Living Land: An Account of the Natural Resources of British Columbia.* Produced by the British Columbia Natural Resources Conference. New York: William Morrow and Company, 1961.

Johnson, Hugh A. "Seward's Folly Can Be a Great Land." Reprinted from 1958 *Yearbook of Agriculture,* Yearbook Separate No. 2923. Washington: Govt. Printing Office, 1958.

———, and Harold T. Jorgenson. *The Land Resources of Alaska.* A Conservation Foundation study. New York: The University Publishers, 1963.

———, and Robert Coffman. *Land Occupancy, Ownership and Use on Homesteads in the Kenai Peninsula, Alaska, 1955.* Alaska Agricultural Experiment Station Bul. No. 21, 1956.

Land Economics Institute. *Modern Land Policy.* Urbana: University of Illinois Press, 1960.

Lang, Herbert C. "Progress in State Land Administration: Selection Policy Considerations," *Science in Alaska 1963.* Proceedings of the Fourteenth Alaskan Science Conference, Anchorage, Alaska, August 27–30, 1963. Alaska Division A.A.A.S., 1964.

Leopold, A. Starker, and F. Fraser Darling. *Wildlife in Alaska.* New York: The Ronald Press Company, 1953.

National Resources Committee. *Regional Planning Part VII—Alaska: Its Resources and Development.* Washington: Govt. Printing Office, 1938.

Owen, Wilfred. *Strategy for Mobility* (Transport Research Program). Washington: The Brookings Institution, 1964.

Public Administration Service. "The Alaskan Constitution and the State Patrimony," *Constitutional Studies,* Vol. 1, Part 3, November 1955.

Rader, Rep. John. "An Explanation of Bill for Incorporation of First Class Organized Boroughs, 1963." (Mimeographed)

"Report to the Secretary of the Interior by the Task Force on Alaska Native Affairs." Report compiled at the request of the Secretary of the Interior by the Task Force on Native Affairs, W. W. Keeler, Chairman, 1962. (Mimeographed)

Riley, Burke. "Federal Land Policy and Its Effect on Development and Settlement in Alaska." A report to the Alaska Development Board, Juneau. Territory of Alaska, 1948. (Mimeographed)

Robinson, Roger R. "BLM and Alaska's Recreation Program." Paper delivered at the A.A.A.S. Alaska Science Conference, Anchorage, Alaska, September 1964. (Mimeographed)

Rogers, George W. *The Future of Alaska: Economic Consequences of Statehood.* Baltimore: The Johns Hopkins Press, 1962.

———, and Richard A. Cooley. *Alaska's Population and Economy: Regional Growth, Development and Future Outlook* (Vol. I, Analysis and Vol. II, Statistical Handbook). University of Alaska Economic Series, Institute of Business, Economic and Government Research, 1963.

Rose, John Kerr. "A Brief Survey of National Policies on Federal Land Ownership." Washington: Library of Congress, 1956. (Mimeographed)

Smith, Richard G. "A Survey of Alaskan Resources Relative to Land Policy." Prepared for Alaska Department of Natural Resources, Division of Lands, May 1963. (Typescript)

Stanley, Kirk W. "Alaska Tidelands: Their Use and Development." Reprint from *Shore and Beach,* October 1962.

State of Alaska. Administrative Code. Title II (Natural Resources); Division I (Lands). (Mimeographed)

———. *Alaska Statutes, Title 38—Public Lands.* Reprint from *Alaska Statutes,* December 1962, as supplemented through 1963. Charlottesville: The Michie Company.

State of Alaska, Department of Administration. "State Revenue Sources Actual and Estimated." Reports for years 1959 through 1964. (1964 report contains projects to 1970.) (Mimeographed)

State of Alaska, Department of Fish and Game. *Annual Report,* 1958 through 1963. Juneau, Alaska.

State of Alaska, Department of Natural Resources, Division of Lands. "Alaska Land Lines" (monthly report on activities 1959 through 1964). (Mimeographed)

The Conservation Foundation. "A Policy Study of Outdoor Recreation Potential in Alaska" (Progress Report). Prepared for Outdoor Recreation Resources Review Commission, Washington, June, 1960. (Mimeographed)

———. "Alaska Program Analysis." Prepared for the U.S. Department of Interior, February 1952. (Mimeographed)

Timmons, John F., and William G. Murray. *Land Problems and Policies.* Ames: The Iowa State College Press, 1950.

Tunnard, Christopher, and Boris Pushkarev. *Man-Made America: Chaos or Control.* New Haven: Yale University Press, 1963.

Udall, Stewart. *The Quiet Crisis.* New York: Holt, Rinehart and Winston, 1963.

U.S. Department of Agriculture. *Land: The Yearbook of Agriculture 1958.* Washington: Govt. Printing Office, 1958.

U.S. Department of Agriculture, Forest Service. "Multiple Use Management Guide for the Alaska Region." Forest Service Handbook. Juneau, Alaska, April 1964. (Mimeographed)

———. "Multiple Use Plan for Admiralty Island North Tongass National Forest." Juneau, Alaska, February 1964. (Mimeographed)

U.S. Department of the Interior. "Land Problem in Alaska Complex," *Annual Report of the Secretary of the Interior,* 1963. Washington: Govt. Printing Office, 1963.

U.S. Department of the Interior, Bureau of Land Management. *BLM at Work in Alaska.* Washington, 1963.

———. *Brief Notes on the Public Domain.* (Revised January 1957.) Washington.

———. *Information Relative to the Use and Disposal of Public Lands and Resources.* Information Bul. No. 2 revised. Washington: Govt. Printing Office, 1957.

———. *Project Twenty-Twelve: A Long Range Program for Our Public Lands.* Washington: Govt. Printing Office, 1960.

———. *Public Land Statistics, 1964.* Washington: Govt. Printing Office, 1964.

U.S. Department of the Interior, Office of the Secretary, Division of Information. *The Race for Inner Space.* Washington: Govt. Printing Office, 1964.

University of California, Agricultural Experiment Station. *Conserving Wildland Resources Through Research.* October 1959.

University of California, Division of Agricultural Sciences. *65 Million Acres of Wildland in California's Future.* Proceedings of the 1959 Wildland Research Center Conference, Yosemite Park, October 19–20, 1959. 1960.

Index

Aboriginal land rights. *See* Native land rights
Access road program: to enhance value of state lands, 60.
Access to public waters. *See* Water access
Acquisition, territorial: of Alaska, 7–8; of federal public domain, 18–19
Administrative Procedures Act (state): requirements for public hearings, 35
Agricultural Experiment Station, 88
Agricultural lands: location of, 16; federal land policies for, 18, 20; state classification of, 39; disposal by state, 51; preference rights to farmers under state law, 52–53; need for policy revisions, 77–78. *See also* Land ownership pattern; Homestead Act (federal); Homesteading program, state
Agriculture, Department of, 22 *n*, 67 *n*, 88
Agriculture, Secretary of: approval of state land selections, 29–30; state land selections in National Forests, 99–100; planning functions in Alaska, 113
Alaska: unspoiled environment of, 3, 8; ecological study of, 5; size of, 7; purchase of, 7; contrasting views on, 8; inadequate knowledge about, 8; physical geography of, 9–11; access to interior, 9–10; natural characteristics of, 9–17; climate of, 11–12; flora and fauna of, 12–14; wildlife resources of, 12–13; mineral production of, 14; geology of, 14–16; mapping of, 15; summary of natural resources, 16; unique pattern of land ownership of, 19; percent of federal lands in, 23–24; strategic military location of, 63; trend in population growth, 64–65, 129
Alaska-Canada border, 10
Alaska Coal Leasing Act (federal), 21
Alaska Field Committee, 109
Alaska Harriman Expedition: description of Alaska, 8
Alaska Land Lines, 52 *n*
Alaska Peninsula, 10, 14
Alaska Railroad, 10
Alaska Range: description of, 10; flora and fauna of, 13
Aleutian Islands, 7, 10; fauna of, 13; grasslands of, 14
Anchorage Daily Times, 127 *n*
Anderson, Clinton P.: functions following earthquake, 111
Arctic: environment, 7, 10, 11; unique characteristics of, 87
Arctic Biology, Institute of, 94
Arctic Circle, 10
Arctic National Wildlife Range, 22
Arctic Ocean, 10, 14
Arctic Research Laboratory, Naval, 94
Arctic Slope, 14; oil explorations on, 15
Army, Department of the, 22 *n*
Arthur D. Little Co., 109
Auction of land: state requirements on, 41, 42, 45, 46–47. *See also* Land disposal, state

Bancroft, H. H.: *History of Alaska,* 7 *n*
Barnett, Harold J.: natural resource scarcity, 123 *n*

Benefit-cost analysis, 126
Bering Sea, 7, 10, 11; climatic influence of, 12; marine mammals of, 13
Boroughs: creation of, 103; land selection authority of, 104; John F. Rader on, 104, 104 *n;* cost of land selections, 105–6; controversy with state, 106–7
Bowman, Wallace D., 89 *n;* Alaska recreation study by, 5
British Columbia, 9, 10; timber export policies of, 103
Brookings Institute, 81
Brooks Range: wildness of, 10, 11: flora and fauna of, 14; oil explorations in, 15
Brown bear: conflict with cattle on Kodiak Island, 83

Caldwell, Lynton K.: on environmental administration, 125–26
Chamberlain, Mount, 10
Chugach National Forest: establishment of, 21. *See also* National Forests
Civil Service System (state): impact on land program, 35
Clarence Rhode Waterfowl Refuge: establishment of, 22
Classification. *See* Land classification
Classification and Multiple Use Act (federal), 97
Clean Air Act (federal), 121
Climate, 11–12
Coal lands: withdrawn from location and entry, 21
Coastline: length of, 7; status of tidelands and submerged lands, 27; erosion of, 61; natural beauty of, 91; industrial sites on, 91. *See also* Tidelands; Submerged lands
Coast Range: description of, 9, 10; climatic influence of, 11
Coffman, Robert: on federal homesteading, 79 *n*
Colville River, 10
Commerce, Department of, 88
Commerce, Secretary of: planning function in Alaska, 113
Commercial lands: state classification of, 39; sale by state, 51
Community expansion and recreation: land grants for, 28; limited by Statehood Act, 29–30; Forest Service and, 99–100. *See also* Land selection, state; Recreation lands
Congressional delegate, territorial: on federal land policies, 24
Conservation: genesis of conservation movement, 19; Alaskan attitude toward, 24–26; provisions in state constitution, 33–34; regulation of oil and gas conservation, 45; relation to state fiscal problems, 67–68; new concept of, 119–30 *passim;* recent federal legislation on, 120–21
Conservation Foundation, the, ix; study of Alaska resources, 4–6; report to Secretary of the Interior, 93–94
Constitution, Alaska: adoption of, 32; natural resource provisions of, 32–34; on borough government, 103
Cook Inlet, 9: oil explorations in, 15
Cooley, Richard A., 5 *n*, 63 *n*
Cooperative Wildlife Research Unit, 94
Coordination, governmental. *See* Planning
Copper River Delta Game Management Area: establishment of, 86. *See also* Game management areas
Corps of Engineers, 22 *n*, 88; tideland studies by, 61
"Country estates:" state land disposals of, 58
Credit allowance program: for state homesteads, 52

Daily Alaska Empire, 69 *n*
Darling, F. Fraser: ecological study of Alaska, 5 *n*
Defense: and Alaska land policy, 23, 30; impact on economy, 63
Defense, Secretary of: planning functions in Alaska, 113
DeLeonardis, Salvatore, 67 *n*
Delta River, 10
Development of state lands: requirement for development plans, 40–41; programs to enhance state land val-

ues, 59–60. *See also* Economic development
Diomede Islands, 7

Earthquake, Alaska: economic influence, 66; impact on tidelands, 93; aftermath of, 111
Ecology: Alaska studies, 5; research needs, 94, 121; ecological perception of environment, 125–26. *See also* Land management
Economic development: contrasting views on, 8; importance of land grant for, 31; objectives of Division of Lands for, 48; use of state lands for, 40–41, 53, 56, 59–60; importance of oil and gas leasing to, 54–55; importance of natural resources to, 56, 65–66; trends in, 62–69; impact of government spending on, 63–64; unemployment problems, 64, 65; outlook for, 65–66; relation to population growth, 124. *See also* Natural Resources; Planning
Economic Development and Planning, Department of (state), 5, 109. *See also* Planning
Egan, William A., Governor of Alaska, 129
Environmental Administration, 126. *See also* Ecology; Land Management
Environmental pollution: growing problems of, 87–88, 119–20; Stewart Udall on, 119; recent congressional action, 120–21; economist's views on, 121–23; impact of population growth, 124; political problems of, 124–26; Alaska evidence of, 127–28. *See also* Esthetic values; Natural beauty
Eskimos: subsistence needs of, 13, 14; land claims of, 74–77
Esthetic values: in land use, 118–19; need for protection of, 84. *See also* Environmental pollution; Natural beauty

Fairbanks, Alaska, 10, 12
Farming: potential for, 16, 79; speculation on state lands, 52–53. *See also* Agricultural lands; Land ownership pattern; Speculation, land
Federal Aviation Agency: planning functions in Alaska, 113
Federal conservation policies. *See* Conservation
Federal Field Committee for Development Planning in Alaska: established by executive order, 113. *See also* Planning
Federal Inter-Agency Committee on Water Resources, 88
Federal lands: extent of, 22–25; percent of total in Alaska, 23–24; controversy over Alaska reserves, 24–25; state selection of, 25–26. *See also* Land management; Land Management, Bureau of; Reservation of lands; and see under specific agencies
Federal Power Commission, 22 *n,* 113
Federal Reconstruction and Development Planning Commission for Alaska: established after earthquake, 111
Fiscal problems, state: importance of land grants, 31; impact of oil and gas leases on, 54–55, 65–66, 67; added costs of statehood, 63, 66–67; in relation to conservation issues, 67–68; lack of funds for research, 90, 95. *See also* Economic development
Fischman, Leonard L., 56 *n,* 122 *n*
Fisher, Joseph, L., 56 *n,* 122, 123 *n*
Fish and Game, Department of (state): water access program of, 58; concerned with impact of logging on fish, 84; protection of fragile wildlife habitats, 84–85; cooperative game management areas, 86–87; attitude toward water code, 87, 88; water coordinator position established, 93; relations with Forest Service, 111. *See also* Fishery resources; Game management areas; Water access; Wildlife resources
Fish and Wildlife Service, U.S., 22, 22 *n,* 23, 88
Fishery resources, 5, 12–14; native use of for subsistence, 13, 76; potential

commercial development, 16; acquisition of land by shore fisheries, 20, 47, 47 *n;* access to sport fisheries, 59; decline of salmon, 65; effect of logging on salmon, 84; conflict over gravel removal, 93. *See also* Water access; Tidelands; Submerged lands

Forest resources, 12, 13, 16, 19; federal reservation of, 21, 23; sale of timber from public domain, 21; management of, 33, 55–56; state classification of timber lands, 38; state requirements for timber sales, 42; lack of knowledge about, 55; state revenues from, 55; state selection of in interior, 55–56; inventory of, 55–56; extent of state timber sales, 56; foreign markets for, 56, 100–3; future importance to state of, 56, 65–66; fire protection for, 56, 70; impact of homesteading on, 97; effects of timber export policies on, 100–3. *See also* Forest Service

Forest Service: lands of, 22, 23; limitations on state land selections, 29–30; effects of logging on salmon, 84; multiple use management plans of, 85, 110–11; cooperation with other government agencies, 86–87, 110–11, water research by, 88; water influence zone established, 92; conflict over state land selections in national forests, 99–100; timber export policies of, 101

Fur resources: state revenues from, 55. *See* Pribilof Islands; Wildlife resources

Galbraith, Kenneth, 121

Game management areas: establishment by state, 85–87; federal-state cooperation on, 86–87. *See also* Wildlife resources

Gannet, Henry: description of Alaska, 8

General Land Office: land disposal policies of, 18, 22 *n*, 24

Geological Survey, U.S., 22 *n*, 88

Geophysical Institute, 94

Glaciers, 9, 10

Gold mining, 11, 65

Governor of Alaska. *See* State government

Gravel: removal from tidelands, 92–93

Gross National Product: as symbol of progress, 122

Grazing lands: extent of, 13, 14, 16; federal leasing policies on, 21; state classification of, 38; conflict on Kodiak Island over, 83

Grazing Service, U.S.; consolidated with General Land Office, 22 *n*

Health and Welfare, Department of (state), 88

Health, Education and Welfare, Secretary of (federal): planning functions in Alaska, 113

Herfindahl, Orris C., 123 *n*

Highway Act, Federal, 70–71

Highway Beautification Act (federal), 121

Highway construction: impact on resource development, 80–82

Highways, Department of (state): relations with other agencies, 57, 81

Hinterlands, 9; difficulties of state selection in, 69–70; native land claims in, 74

Homestead Act (federal), 118: extended to Alaska, 20; original intent of, 42, 78; special provisions for native homesteads, 75; need for revision, 77–78, 97. *See also* Agricultural lands; Land ownership pattern

Homesteading, state program for: constitutional provisions on settlement, 34; provisions for, 42–43; improvement credit system, 43; classification and sale of homesteads, 52–53; preference rights to, 52–53; need for revision of policies on, 77–78. *See also* Agricultural lands; Homestead Act, U.S.; Land ownership pattern

Housing and Home Finance Agency: planning functions in Alaska, 113

Hydroelectric dams: potential for, 16; consideration of fish and wildlife values, 87–88

Hydroelectric sites: reservation of, 21; mining in, 22 *n*, Rampart Dam withdrawal, 22
Hydrological data: gathering of, 88–89

Icefields, 9
Indian Affairs, Bureau of, 22, 23, 72–77
Indians: subsistence needs of, 13; reservations for, 23; land claims of, 74–77
Industrial lands: state classification of, 39
Industry. *See* Economic development
"In-place" land grants: abandonment of in Statehood Act, 27
Institute of Business, Economic and Government Research, 5 *n*, 63, 94
Interagency coordinating committees, 115. *See also* Planning
Inter-agency Technical Committee for Alaska: collects hydrological data, 88–89
Interior, Department of the: program analysis of, 4, 5, 5 *n;* resource agencies of, 22 *n;* and native land claims, 74–75; water research functions, 88; Alaska Field Committee of, 109
Interior, Secretary of the, 4, 19, 29; report on native affairs to, 75–77; planning functions in Alaska, 109, 113
Izembek Waterfowl Refuge (federal), 22

Japan: market for Alaska timber, 56, 100–3
Johnson, Hugh A., 6, 79 *n*
Johnson, President Lyndon, 111; message on natural beauty, 119–20
Jorgenson, Harold T., 6 *n*
Juneau, Alaska, 11–12

Kenai National Moose Range, 84
Kenai Peninsula, 9, 53, 61
Kennedy, President John F., 112
Klondike, Yukon Territory, 11
Kneese, Allen V., 123 *n*
Kobuk River, 10
Kodiak Island, 9; cattle and brown bear conflict, 83
Kotzebue, 10
Koyukuk River, 10
Kuskokwim River, 11, 13

Labor, Secretary of: planning functions in Alaska, 113
Lambert, Darwin, 69 *n*
Land Act, Alaska: highlights of, 35; patenting of tidelands under, 46; on land reserves for single-purpose use, 85
Land and Water Conservation Fund Act, 89–90, 120
Land classification: basis of state authority, 35, 37–40; of timber lands, 38; provisions for reclassification, 40; procedures for state classification, 40–41; for oil and gas leasing, 45 *n;* of tide and submerged lands, 46–47, 61, 91; amount classified by state, 51; of homestead units, 52; of state recreation areas, 56–57; of wildlife habitats, 84–85; Bureau of Land Management authority, 96–99
Land disposal: of federal public domain lands in West, 18–19. *See also* Speculation, land
Land disposal, state: public hearings on, 35, 58; prior classification of, 40–41; lease and sale provisions, 40–42; acreage limitations on, 41; procedural safeguards for, 41, 58; appraisal requirements, 41; installment purchase provisions for, 41, 51, 52; public auction requirements, 41, 42, 45, 46–47; oil and gas leasing regulations, 44–46, 53–55; leasing of tide and submerged lands, 46–47, 61; shore fishery leasing, 47 *n;* survey of land, 50–51; demand for land, 51–52; speculation on, 51–53; of homesteads, 52–53; revenues from, 53; of timber, 56; of "country estates," 58; land credit certificates, 60; promotion by state of, 60–61
Land grant, Alaska: provisions in early statehood bills, 25; Alaska Statehood Act on, 25–31; Alaska grant compared to other states, 25–27; Submerged Land Act, 27; estimated

total grant, 28; congressional intent of, 31; economic and fiscal importance of, 31, 54–55, 66–68. *See also* Mental health land grant; School land grant; University land grant

Land management: controversy over federal policies, 18–25, 33, 97; state Administrative Procedures Act on, 35; state timber management plans, 55–56; costs of to state government, 55 *n*, 70–72; Forest Service management plans, 85, 110–11; ecology of land management, 94, 125–26. *See also* Lands, Division of; Multiple use; State government

Land Management, Bureau of: formation of, 22 *n;* lands of, 22, 23; disagreement with state, 49, 97; transfer of campgrounds to state, 57; classification authority of, 96–99; appropriations for development programs in Alaska, 98–99; timber export policies of, 101

Land ownership pattern, 9, 19–24, 27, 34, 37, 80–81. *See also* Land selection; Land disposal

Land reserves. *See* Reservation of land

Land revenues, state: from federal lands to state, 31, 35; from oil and gas leasing, 46, 53–54, 66–67; from land lease and sale, 53, 55; importance of to state government, 48, 66–68; and cost of state land selections, 71–72. *See also* Economic development; Fiscal problems; Land disposal, state

Lands, Division of: creation of, 35; organization of, 36; regulatory policies of, 37; powers of, 47; objectives of, 48–49; accomplishments of, 48–62, 108; relations with other government agencies, 48–49, 99–100, 103–4; land disposals of, 51–52; parks program of, 57; timber export policies of, 101. *See also* Land classification; Land disposal; Land selection, state

Landsberg, Hans H., 56 *n*, 122 *n*

Land selection, state: provisions governing, 24–31; Statehood Act on, 29; relation to national defense, 30; costs of, 30, 56, 66–67, 70–72, 105–6; location of, 49; existing selections, extent of, 49, 51; federal-state conflicts over, 49, 50, 69–70, 74–75, 97–99, 100; of interior forest lands, 55–56; problems of, 49, 69–70; research needs for, 70; challenged by native land claims, 74–75; selections for recreation program, 90; "defensive" selections, 97; conflict with Forest Service over, 99–100; conflict with borough governments over, 103–7. *See also* Community expansion and recreation

Land settlement: state constitutional policy on, 32–33; state requirements for homesteading, 42–43; problems of, 73–82; social costs of, 79. *See also* Agricultural lands; Homestead Act (federal); Homesteading program, state; Land Ownership pattern

Land speculation. *See* Speculation, land

Land survey. *See* Survey, land

Lang, Herbert C., 67 *n*, 72 *n*

Lease of land. *See* Land disposal, state

Leopold, A. Starker, 5 *n*

Logging, effect on salmon resources, 84

Mackenzie River, 10

Malaspina Glacier, 9

Mapping: geological, 15; topographic, 15. *See also* Survey, land

Marine Sciences, Institute of, 94

Matanuska River, 9

Material lands, state classification of, 38

McKinley, Mount, 10

Mental health land grant: provisions for, 25; extent of grant, 28; oil and gas leasing on, 45

Michelson, Mount, 10

Migratory birds. *See* Waterfowl

Military: land reserves of, 23; defense policy and state land selections, 30; impact on Alaska's economy, 63

Mineral Industry Research Laboratory, 94

Mineral lands, 14, 16; coal lands withdrawn from entry, 21; federal-state differences over, 30; state leasing provisions, 30; surface use of, 33; state classification of, 37–38; state control over use of, 40; state policy on exploration, 44; state regulation of, 44–46; state revenues from, 54–56. *See also* Oil and gas

Mineral Leasing Act (federal), 45

Mines, Bureau of (federal), 22 *n*

Mining: importance of, 14, 15, 65; and water resources, 87. *See also* Economic development

Mining laws (federal) extended to Alaska, 20; leasing provisions, 43–45; need for revision, 44, 98, 120

Morse, Chandler: on natural resource scarcity, 123 *n*

Mountain ranges, 9–11

Multiple use: problems of, 16, 126; of mineral lands, 30, 35; state constitutional provisions for, 33; state powers in determining uses, 47; conflicts of on state lands, 84; Forest Service approach to, 85, 110–11; need for research into, 90–91, 94; and Bureau of Land Management, 98

Municipalities: rights to tidelands, 46. *See also* Boroughs; Tidelands

National forests. *See* Forest resources; Forest Service

National parks and monuments, 19, 21, 23

National Resources Committee, 108. *See also* Planning

National Wild Rivers Preservation System, proposed, 121

Native Affairs, Federal Task Force on, 75–77

Native Allotment Act, Alaska (federal), 73, 75, 76–77

Native land rights: problems presented by, 73–77; congressional indecision on, 74; effects on oil and gas exploration, 74–75

Native reservations, 22, 23, 76, 77

Native Townsite Act, Alaska (federal), 74

Natural beauty, 3, 16, 33, 91, 92; new emphasis on, 119–20; President's message on, 120; White House Conference on, 120. *See also* Environmental pollution; Esthetic values

Natural resources: future of, 16, 65–66; inadequate knowledge of, 8, 70, 108; native use for subsistence, 12–14, 72–77; waste of in West, 19; state constitutional policy for, 33–34; national demands for, 56; need for inventories of, 70; impact of highway program on, 60, 80–82; state promotional efforts for, 65–66; role of technology in development of, 122. *See also* Economic development; Fishery resources; Forest resources; Mineral lands; Oil and gas; Recreation resources; Research needs; Water resources; Wildlife resources

Natural Resources, Department of (state), 34, 49 *n*, 88. *See also* Lands, Division of; State government

Navigable waters, 20. *See also* Water access

Nenana River, 10

New York Times, 119

Noatak River, 10

Northern Forest Experiment Station, 94

North Pole, 7

North Slope Native Association: land claims of, 74

Northwest Ordinance, 118

Northern Wildland Research Center: recommendation for, 94

Oil and gas: exploration and development, 14, 15; inferred reserves, 16; petroleum reserves, 23; federal leasing regulations, 44–46; state leasing of, 45–46, 53–55; regulation of well drilling by the state, 45; leases on submerged lands, 45; state incentives for exploration and discovery, 45–46; economic importance of, 65–66; revenues to state from, 46, 66–67; influence of native land claims on explo-

ration, 74–75; conflict with moose, 84. *See also* Land disposal; Land revenues; Mineral lands; Mining
Oil and Gas Conservation Act (state): regulation of well drilling, 45
Omnibus Act, Alaska (federal), 28
Ordway, Samuel H., Jr., 4
Organic Act of 1884, 20
Outdoor recreation. *See* Esthetics; Natural beauty; Recreation resources; Parks
Outdoor Recreation, Bureau of, 22 *n*, 89–90, 120
Outdoor Recreation Council, Alaska, 89
Outdoor Recreation Resources Review Commission, 5, 5 *n*, 89
Owen, Wilfred, 81

Parks: National parks in Alaska, 22 *n*, 23; state aims, 48; state progress in establishment of, 56–57; highway wayside program, 57; limited state funds for, 57. *See also* Recreation resources
Pedestrian easements: state program along streams, 59. *See also* Water access
Permafrost, 11, 14
Petroleum reserves, 23. *See also* Reservation of lands
Petroleum resources. *See* Oil and gas
Pinchot, Gifford, 19
Planning: federal-state relations for, 24, 82, 86–87, 108–9; recent developments in, 110–16. *See also* Alaska Field Committee; Federal Reconstruction and Development Planning Commission for Alaska; Federal Field Committee for Development Planning for Alaska; Interagency coordinating committees; National Resources Board; Planning, Division of (state); President's Review Committee for Development Planning in Alaska
Planning, Division of (state), 109–10
Point Barrow, Alaska, 7, 12
Point Hope, Alaska, 10
Population, 5; trends in, 64–65, 129; native, 75; and economic growth, 124
Power Commission, Public, 113. *See also* Hydroelectric sites
Power reserves, 23. *See also* Hydroelectric sites
President's Review Committee for Development Planning in Alaska, 113. *See also* Planning
Pribilof Islands, 13; state revenues from, 55
Private lands: extent of in Alaska, 21, 23. *See also* Land disposal; Land ownership pattern; Land settlement
Prospecting: state program for, 44–45; permits for, 44 *n*. *See also* Mineral lands; Mining; Oil and gas
Public domain, federal: acquisition of, 7, 18, 19; extent of in Alaska, 22–25. *See also* Land Management, Bureau of
Public hearings. *See* Administrative Procedures Act (state)
Public Health Service, 88
Public Land Law Review Commission, x, 98, 120
Public Land Sale Act (federal), 107 *n*
Public Roads, Bureau of, 88. *See also* Highway Act, Federal

Quantity land grants: substituted for "in place" land grants in Statehood Act, 29

Rader, John, State Representative: on borough land selections, 104, 104 *n*. *See also* Boroughs
Rampart Dam proposal: power site reserved for, 22; controversy over, 87
Range lands. *See* Grazing lands
Reclamation Act (federal), 7 *n*, 31 *n*
Reclamation, Bureau of, 22 *n*, 88
Recreation resources, 5, 21; federal sites transferred to state, 28; state selection and classification of, 38, 39, 56–58, 90; objectives of Division of Lands, 48; sale of by state, 51; state

program for wilderness estates, 58; recreation trails preserved by state, 58–59; growing importance of, 79–80; need for joint planning for, 89, 90; research needs, 90–91; value of tidelands for, 91–92. *See also* Parks; Water access
Reindeer: conflicts with other resources, 84
Research needs: tidelands, 61, 91–92, 93; for resource inventories, 70, 82; in settling multiple-use conflicts, 83–95; water resources, 88; recreation, 90; limitation of state funds for, 90, 95; in ecology of land management, 94, 121, 125–26; role of University of Alaska, 94–95; recommendations of the National Resources Committee, 108
Reservation of lands: federal reserves established, 21–25; attitude in Alaska toward, 24; state policy on, 33, 85; impact of federal reserves on state land program, 69–70. *See also* Conservation; Game management areas; Petroleum reserves; Rampart Dam proposal
Reserved use lands: state classification of, 39
Residential lands: federal acts on, 21; state classification of, 40; sale of by state, 51; country estates, 58
Resources. *See* Natural resources
Resources for the Future, Inc., 56 *n*, 122–23, 127 *n*
Revenue. *See* Land revenues
Richardson Highway, 10
Rivers of Alaska, 9–11
Roads. *See* Highway construction; Access road program
Robinson, Joan, 124
Rockefeller, John D., III, 118
Rocky Mountains, 10
Rogers, George W., 5 *n*, 63 *n*, 79–80
Roosevelt, Theodore, 19
Russia: Alaska acquisition from, 18

St. Elias Mountains, 9
Sale of land. *See* Land disposal, state
School lands, 25, 28. *See also* University land grant
Settlement policies. *See* Agricultural lands; Homestead Act (federal); Homesteading program, state; Land ownership pattern
Seward, William H., 7, 8, 11
Small Business Administration, 113
Soil Conservation Service, 88
Speculation, land, 19, 20, 21, 51, 52–53
Standard Oil Company, 53
Stanley, Kirk W., 47 *n*
State government: organization of, 34, 35; fiscal problems of, 55, 63, 66–67, 81. *See also* Fiscal problems; Lands, Division of; Planning
Statehood Act, 3, 21, 99; land grant provisions of, 25–31; land selections under, 29–30; mineral leasing under, 30–31, 55; and land revenues, 31; accomplishments since passage, 32–47; size of selection units under, 49–50; federal money grants, 66; and costs of statehood, 66–67
Stikine River Waterfowl Management Area, 86. *See also* Game management areas
Subarctic, 11, 87. *See also* Arctic
Submerged lands: ownership of, 27; and federal act, 27; extent of in Alaska, 28; and state constitution, 34; oil and gas leasing on, 45–46; state administration of, 46–47. *See also* Tidelands
Subsistence use areas, proposal for, 13, 76
Survey, land: extent of in Alaska, 20, 29–30; federal-state disagreement over, 49–50; financial burden of, 50–51. *See also* Fiscal problems; Mapping
Susitna River, 9
Sustained-yield management: state constitutional policy, 33; state forest lands, 56

Taylor Grazing Act, 96
Tidelands, 20, 27, 28; state constitutional policy, 34; oil and gas leasing

on, 45; rights of municipalities to, 46; shore fisheries on, 46, 47 *n;* state administration of, 46–47, 61, 91; upland owners' right to, 47; adjudication of private preference rights, 61; erosion of, 61, 93; need for inventory and appraisal of, 61, 91–93; industrial sites on, 91–92; recreational importance of, 91–92; removal of gravel from, 92–93. *See also* Coastline; Fishery resources; Submerged lands
Tikchik Lakes area, 91
Timber export policies: controversy over, 100–3. *See also* Forest resources
Timber lands. *See* Forest resources
Tongass National Forest, 21. *See also* National Forests
Trade and Manufacturing Sites Act (federal), 20

Udall, Stewart, 69, 87, 119
University land grant, 28, 45
University of Alaska, 5 *n,* 63, 94–95
U.S. Congress, 24: land grants to Alaska, 25–26; on tidelands, 27; and native land rights, 74–77; recent conservation legislation of, 121
Utility lands, 40, 51

Valdez, Alaska, 10

Water access: federal protection of, 20; state provisions for, 33, 58; to tidelands, 46–47; Department of Fish and Game program for, 59; access to streams with sport fisheries, 59; reservation of trails to access sites, 59; use of pedestrian easements by state, 59; emerging conflicts over, 87–88
Waterfowl, 13; federal refuges for, 22, 23; cooperative federal-state program for habitat protection, 86. *See also* Game management areas; Wildlife resources
Water influence zones, 92
Water Pollution Laboratory, Federal: in Alaska, 94
Water Quality Act (federal), 121
Water resources, 16, 19; conflicts over, 87–89; research needs, 88
Water Resources Planning Act (federal), 121
Water Resources Research Act (federal), 120
Watershed lands: state classification of, 39
Weather Bureau, 88
Wengert, Norman, 115–16
White House Conference on Natural Beauty, 120
Wickersham, James (territorial delegate): on federal land policies, 24
Wilderness Act, 120
Wilderness estates: state program for, 58
Wilderness resources, 3, 10, 58; importance of to state, 84, 87; management research needs, 94
Wildlands, research uses in Alaska, 94
Wildlife ranges and refuges (federal), 21, 23
Wildlife resources, 12–13; native use of, 75–77; economic importance of, 84; habitat protection for, 84–85, 85–87; conflict with hydroelectric developments, 87–88
Wood River-Tikchik Lakes area: as potential state park, 91
Walrus Islands: first state game sanctuary, 85 *n*

Yukon River, 10, 11, 13; Rampart Dam site on, 22

Zoning, 40, 107 *n;*